MILK HORSES:
A Memoir

For Henry and Betty
This time a book of prose
We wouldn't be who we are
today if it hadn't been for
you.
 always love
  Becky → John

BOOKS BY REBECCA NEWTH

- Poetry: Xeme
   A Journey Whose Bones Are Mine
- Finding the Lamb
- The Oseberg Skiff
- Great North Woods
- Nineteen Poems

MILK HORSES:
A MEMOIR

BY
Rebecca Newth
Rebecca Newth

Lost Creek Press
Fayetteville 1998

Copyright© 1998 by Rebecca Newth
All rights reserved
Printed in the United States of America

01   00   99   98   4   3   2   1

This book was designed by Chang-hee H. Russell / C.R.Graphics
Cover horse photo by Kim Harington

No part of this book may be reproduced or transmitted in any form or by any means, electronic or mechanical, including photocopy, recording or any information storage or retrieval system, without the express written permission of the publisher, except where permitted by law.

Library of Congress Cataloging-in-Publication Data   98-85089

Newth, Rebecca, 1940
   A Memoir
      Michigan, Lansing   Crete   World War II

ISBN 0-9664290-0-1

*with thanks to Jan Trumbo
for encouragement
- and to the Contadina lady*

Acknowledgment

Grateful acknowledgment is made to the editors and publishers of books and magazines in which much of the contents of this volume first appeared: Epiphany, The Grapevine, Satchel, Nimrod, Great North Woods, The Oseberg Skiff (Will Hall Books), Finding the Lamb (Station Hill Press)

Contents

Milk Horses - 1945   *3*

Inside the Lead Mines   *7*

The Bull Fighter   *11*

Tramps   *14*

An Autobiographical Fragment   *19*

The Puff Ball   *31*

A Good Winter Coat   *36*

Miss Gostelow: Teacher of Piano   *46*

The Dreams of My Father   *55*

Tirade   *67*

Aunt Mildred's Bike   *70*

The First Boy   *73*

I'll Never Leave You 85
Ernest Hemingway Died 90
Marie-Cone 97
The Reindeer Boy 107
The Dreams of My Mother 116
Kicks 124
House of Sky 131
Epilogue 139

Milk Horses:
A Memoir

Milk Horses
1945

A horse had been let loose on our street and I was studying it at the curb and wondering how it came there. There was no one to tell me the names of the parts or about the bridle and harness. I would have liked to know what the names were from hoof to ear. Why was the horse here? What did he do at night? Who took care of him? All those questions.

The horse stood at curbside and went to the bathroom. He got hungry and ate with a loud noise. He quivered. He seemed to ask, "Why do we harness a horse?" "Only because there is an intelligence, a witness to watch it," I answered. "That there be a vigilance."

ঽ ঽ ঽ

Why harness a horse? The question needed an answer: an upper story, a thinking room, which it had. In our attic someone had placed a stack of Life *magazines. The question needed also a basement and a yard with a sandbox and hollyhocks and a mother who was sad. The question needed an absent father and circus animals. And an answer must be written because the child liked the mother and wanted to share her nap. But the mother had shut the door, so, instead, the child went to the attic, to the magazines.*

"What do you need?" she asked them.

"One streak of black smoke," they answered. "One small plane."

I am that child.

ঽ ঽ ঽ

On the underside of the world, the Chinese hung from their feet with their pigtails flapping in their faces. And between their feet emerged the roots of our Anglo-Saxon world, much cruder, that contrasted with the delicate chefs and gardeners of the kingdom of China.

Milk Horses–1945

I believed that in this other world, the people were more mannerly, more careful, thoughtful than we. That would account for the whirling sickness of our war. I imagined the Chinese in a fair world where things were clean and peaceful.

The milk horse that came down our street–perhaps he was merely large and not a draft horse–was brown, or black, with a large head and wide lumps over his eyes and small crescents of pink flesh and milky eyeballs tinged with red, and flippy ears alert and waving, one going north and one west, and a harness, a bridle, and a special brass ball for ornament and sometimes a braided or fancy bridle–but here, no, the horse that brought the milk had nothing fancy. Its droppings mixed with grain that came down onto the pavement to the sparrows' delight. The horse had no care for what went on near its tail but only for what concerned the head. Feed bag. The horse, with head in the feed bag and wearing blinders of black leather with silver although he had promised not to break, not to shy at newspapers, feels the blinders at all times and will not break away and run or frighten or stagger and cannot look right or left to the horizon, or the sun or our house but only front or down. The feed bag down. The sparrows down. Our pavement is down. The horse sees down only from an extension of his neck, although he has promised that no boy or bike or dog should ever scare him. But they take precautions. They think he will need the blinders.

I come to see the horse and his strange walk into our morning, the horse tamely down our street from out of nowhere, of no stable into no barn, whose quest began on the rim of Jenesen Street and continued to Willow and then was folded into the day.

Whip. This horse who has no need of blinders much less a whip. I run out to see the horse though he cannot look side to side and acknowledge me. Yet, he knows I am there. I am embarrassed when I see the whip. I see also the bit in the teeth and the idea for fitting the horse's weakness–his mouth–for the cart. I see his haunches, which things sparrows love, and the sun. All this, and my mother gets the morning milk.

The horse's skin shivers; its flesh quivers hoof to hoof. Now this. Now that. This one. Now that one. Noon droops upon the horse, the day's standstill with no shadow. Pressed weight here, there, this one, that one. Our milk. Feed bag. Whip. Cart of white. Horse, in no shade. On Jenesen.

I wonder about the size of bone in the leg, about the joints. I see up close, very clearly, a blood vein. This immense creature has the same body I have. We share veins. Then commences the play of the tail. The family of flies begin it, so that the tail is like a careless out-flying in advance like a paper boy's cast. Yet none of the flies drops, none is so much as stunned. Flesh creeps, flies, bodies–it is the stamping of legs, the tail, nose. Acquaintanceship with the long sanded expanse, the dusty shuddering, noise of wind through wide upper lip nuzzling. Stamp. Slap. Crunch of grain.

Finally, I leave the pavement and cross the lawn to the backyard. The sight of the horse gradually leaves me. I go under a tree. I am amazed, but I would not want to be him.

ᛉ ᛉ ᛉ

In the afternoon my mother goes into her bedroom to nap and the day hangs heavy. I have made all the dolls I can out of hollyhocks and have spied on all the bees and ants. I sneak upstairs to the attic to get the magazines. There, I quickly turn pages looking for the children–the horse still upon me in spirit–turning page after page by myself and peeking at some more closely, according to fate.

On the cover of one is a marine in full spread before a blazing sunset. I look in the contents for something about "Jews". There is nothing. I look for "Concentration Camps" or "Internment Camps". Then I find something called "World War II Atrocities". It is a strange route. I go through most of that Life *magazine.*

I am confronted by a picture of Emmet Kelley, the Ringling Brothers' clown, rushing to pour a pail of water on the Big Top. I see, also, bombing pictures, an article about a retired soldier with one arm, pictures of the Presidential Convention–Dewey and Truman–pictures of Teddy Roosevelt's funeral, aerial views by Margaret Bourke-White. There are articles on the discovery of penicillin, on gypsy moths, on Dutch Elm Disease and the advent of television which is billed as part of the radio industry, and then there is a picture of Henry Ford hoeing a field of wheat.

I remember, in particular, a picture of three women, released inmates from a French insane asylum. Wearing dresses, they stand in the middle of a road, in front of a house with a charred roof that has burned so completely that now the rafters are coming through. A man is motioning to another woman to come up the front walk. Is she going to enter the charred house? Will the women from the insane asylum have a place to go in? Are they all turned loose on roads that lead nowhere?

And then, I read of the children shot by the Gestapo and fed to circus animals.

&   &   &

At four mother's face has sleep on it and her eyes look sad. There is nothing to do. The day, still some of it remains. She comes downstairs with the marks of sleep on her face. On my face there are the traces of the magazines. What should we do, I wonder. If only the day would melt. It seems to proceed, insult after insult, by devils, first one and then another and by the casting out of them, and even now it is only four o'clock.

I go outside to the sandbox. "I believe in God even when He is silent", one of the inscriptions in the Life magazine read.

The horse has long gone. He was not like me; I did not really understand him either. But I had wished him for a friend.

And then I began to feel tears come and to produce them cost me—my throat and eyes had scarcely room for them and they were bodies, too, like the children that didn't matter.

INSIDE THE LEAD MINES

We did not really have lead mines in Lansing; it only seemed so to me. In the part of town where we lived, the sidewalks were old and buckled, the trees filthy and heavy, the leaves seeming to be polluted. Children who lived in the old houses with tricycles parked on the porch were said to have 'cooties'. We said lots of things had cooties. I thought cooties were a kind or ring-worm, but I knew it must mean something more. Cooties: the official name for something microscopic that looked, up close, like an anteater, and whose name could serve as an insult.

In this town, Malcolm X's father, their name was Little, was run-over by a trolley car, some thought he was placed on the tracks, and Stevie Wonder went to the Michigan School for the Blind, which was across from my school.

The street we lived on was old and narrow, the houses dusty on the outside, the people in them unfriendly. The woman who lived across the street told me she put on lipstick to make her lips look like my mother's.

She said, "Your mother has the most perfect lips I have ever seen."

I was horrified. If only my mother knew. I should tell her. She always thought her mouth was ugly. (She had crooked teeth). What would she think? She would think the woman had spoken out of line.

The kids at school frightened me, the days frightened me. We had air raids. We were supposed to be looking out for Japanese planes with red circles on them. Our newspapers were full of war. Our radios hummed of it. My father had no car and had to ride a bike to work and we had to squeeze oleo. We saved blue and red chips for rationing and my mother, the only woman anyone knew whose seams were not crooked, couldn't get nylons.

We used to walk to the market every afternoon. It was four blocks away, all of them dark and rugged and I always fell and scratched up my knee and when we arrived at last, with the baby, and me with a bleeding knee, and my mother looking like a movie star except for her teeth, we bought a few things and just turned around again and came back down those four filthy blocks to our small bungalow where my father would come and where I bade my time with my very young parents.

'One day is good, the next day is bad' that's how I saw it. After a while I amended that to 'one day good, two days bad.' The day I got stuck in the mud was the 'off' day, the bad day anyhow. I should have known. I could have stayed inside that day, after school, but no, I had gone out to play across the street in a vacant, muddy lot. I remember I stuck one foot into the mud to test it and it would not come out. And then I put the other one in and felt the first go deeper. I was stuck. I tugged on both my legs. I couldn't lift my feet. I couldn't even turn around. I was rooted.

And how would it look? Here I was, a child standing by the sidewalk in Lansing, Michigan and this girl was stuck in mud.

"Look, mommy. That little girl can't get out, I bet'cha!"

This had never happened to anyone, never anyone wearing Grandma's gift of a raincoat and standing all alone in the rain after a day in school which had had its own horrors. No, and after all that, I had to come outside and step in some mud.

As it happened, my mother didn't look out to check on me and I didn't want anyone else to notice, so finally with a mighty effort, I made several quick, shuffling movements with my feet in rapid order so that my weight went from one boot to the other one before the mud KNEW,

And then with gasping sucks and gurgles I was able to heave one lumpish foot to the curb and then the other. I was peppered with mud! I was a pauper of mud.

There had been the time I got on the bus with my mother and turned my legs cross-wise on the seat and a big woman got on and sat down on them. I went home. The house was silent. I let the outside sink into its dismal and disgusting night. I might find my books, touch the shined and loved illustrations, the silvered dogs and children, umbrellas, the muffin-sit-before-the-fireside children of all my books whose words I loved. They might talk of war, but I had my books. They might talk of B-25 bombers–my grandfather especially–they might talk, but I had my long hedge beside which the world must pass.

Would I be allowed to grow up, and use those words? When I did try to use them I mangled it so badly, I wrote worse than people who didn't even care, who didn't try.

This amused my mother when I told her this. But that was okay for her. As for me, I would someday fly, I would ordain paper, I would stain the glancing air, I would remove myself. Most of all, I would get out of the lead mines.

I loved the stories read to us during the last half hour of school and especially the last fifteen minutes, hated the beginning school day, the flag, the standing, the sitting, the lunch, the recess (oh God) and then again another recess and the lockers and the near end the blessed near end coming coming near end it was almost time the lights flickering the dawning adored smell of eraser–numb middle finger, with the lump, smelling of scissors–near end and, "Put your heads down, and don't look, and the cheater must raise his hand," near end, end.

One Christmas as I was standing on the old spavined sofa in order to look out the windows that reflected the tree, I saw four panes of glass and a scarlet ball with white panes and then Roosevelt died of a headache. It was as if the street and school and Christmas conjoined with the President's death; and my mother did nothing, said nothing about it. She wore her nylons with the seams and my father was still in the Civil Defense.

The wonder of a blackened room, the wonder of illness to a child. This was the time of childhood illness, of feverish dreams, of the start of penicillin. The wonder to a child of a woman lying in a bathtub, the dark dividing line running mysteriously from crotch to navel. The wonder, to a child, of the approaching long-run of education—of enclosure and division, male and female, teacher and student. The wonder of the things the fairy tales hint at: knees of stone head of bone poetry. And it was eight years before they sent me to a piano teacher to learn the muffled chords of this cold world, somebody's paradise, for sure, but whose? I could not imagine.

Lying nude on a bed, no doubt, with her legs crossed. A woman of leisure, like my mother, with the newspaper, and when? That purple time just before evening when everything is unfocused, the whole day in disarray. Nobody knows what to do. There is the meal to be gotten, the table to be set. The nap is over, lights are not on, and it is strange, hard to keep on the move.

Heck! I would say. If there IS a woman in paradise in that lost time just before evening and she IS lying on a bedspread, why did she not tell me a story, welcome me? Why, if God is a man (and he is not) or if God is a woman (and he is not) or if God is a person, why, then didn't someone put a glass prism in my hand, hold it up to the light, show me the pestling of first and last times?

It was evening, and I saw at the end of the lawn, black hedges, the cherry tree where my mother had stood on a stool and gathered the fruit and pitted the cherries, staining her hands the color of mahogany.

The Bull Fighter

I was the oldest child. My birth was followed by a miscarriage when I was two and by the birth of a brother when I was four. He was too young to play with and I needed someone to talk to. Later on, I had a second brother and then a sister but that was when I had to start raising myself because of my parents.

I would talk you to death, my mother reported. But, at the same time, I was so shy that relatives feared I could never be induced to go to school, not that there was any choice.

My relationship to my mother, the birth of my brother, books– these were the important things. I had no friends except for Sarah Jane. My dolls were consequently named Sarah's baby, Sarah Jane, or, Grandpa's baby, and so forth. In addition, I had an imaginary playmate whom I talked to out loud and she was really also Sarah Jane.

I never could tell my parents that I loved them or that I was sorry for anything I did or that I needed them to do something. I always wanted them to touch my hair but I dared not ask. Once in a while my mother's hand would stray to my hair and this would be heaven. But I had to remain absolutely still so no one would guess how much I needed it.

When finally I went to school, I developed leg aches and could not see the black board. Being nearsighted, a problem which neither of my parents discovered until I was in third grade–in church, I strained to see to the rafters. I puzzled over the symbols in the wood, the clover leaf, the triangle. My eyes went over them, the unending riddle mixed with grape leaves. Jesus' face. Lansing, Michigan had laid hold of a few of these old and original pictures. "We might be shut-in to the inside of the country," I thought, "away from the ports and centers of trade, but we have secreted in our churches (and in our schools) a few symbols, some harmonies."

It was fitting that across the street from my school there was a chicken hatchery because we were not so very sophisticated in Lansing. I watched the windows every day to see if any eggs hatched. The windows were grey and dirty. Sometimes a whole window-full of chicks, all yellow, were born. Near that factory was the Fisher Body plant where my grandpa worked, that had made parts for bombers.

One day I saw a movie about a Spanish bull fighter. There were the silks, the colors, and the famous way the bull fighter made the passes with his cape. I was entranced with it. I went home and from a band uniform of my father's I made my own cape and hurled it. I waved the bull through. I tarnished the silks in the dirt. I lay the cape over the fence of my sandbox and pulled threads in it. However, I had no one to play the bull. And one day Justin came into my yard.

Justin was a muddy boy who ran around the neighborhood like a forgotten dog. He lived down the way around the block in a white house. He had a grandmother. One day he appeared in the yard. I thought immediately that he might do for the bull. He had a fascinating scab–sort of like a piece of ham. I told him about the movie, how the bull must run past the bull fighter while the bull fighter puts the cape in front of it. And when the bull makes a pass the bull must seem to charge directly at the bullfighter but in fact the bullfighter lets the cape, and the bull, pass near his hip.

"The bull is going for the color red, the red cape," I explained.

"Awright," said Justin who spoke loudly. He didn't merit going up in my tree house. He was mean to ants and crushed them with his fingers. I got popsicles from the refrigerator for him and he let them melt all over his face. When he first went to play the bull, he put his head down and didn't run the right way. He would either run in another direction or he would run too far away from the cape.

I had to give him the cape and pretend I was the bull to show him how. But he was too impatient to stand still.

"Don't move," I ordered him. "Hold the cape like this across your hip and pretend the bull is going for your groin. Now at the last moment lead the bull to one side."

"Ah, sure," Justin said. He spoke few words but really didn't understand things. He took aim, ran back and then ran right at me with his hard head down and blasted me right in the stomach. I fell, rolling in pain and he laughed and laughed because he had run at me even when I diverted him with the cape. "What's wrong?" he asked, as if he didn't know. I was furious. What kind of a person would do that?

"I'll do it again, I'll do it again," he promised, "and this time I'll do it right."

"No, you won't," I said. He'd had enough trouble watching for Japanese planes, Justin always thinking any sound was an engine, any wing had round circles. I decided I would rather be alone than have Justin in my yard.

"You can go on home," I told him.

"Naw," he said. "Don't want to."

Then I thought of bribing him with a popsicle. I ran in and asked my mother, "Can I have an orange popsicle for that boy, Justin?" She was standing there as if the day had no bullfighters in it. She probably thought I had been playing and talking outloud to the imaginary Sarah Jane—but she gave me one.

Tramps

At the end of our street was a woods and tramps came to it. I say this because we knew they roamed the country on trains. There was an active track that ran from Kalamazoo straight to our water tower in Lansing. We heard these trains at night. The tracks were stark and amongst them were pieces of metal and paper. The tramps came from some other place. It was likely, if you were one of the big kids and parked with your boyfriend at the end of the road where it met the track, that you would run into a tramp.

The dividing line between tramps and regular people was this: tramps were untrustworthy vagrants who moved around without ever stopping. The question I asked myself was: "Why did they want to come to Lansing?"

We were confined to one side of the woods by a creek. Our side contained more trees and was generally uncleared of brush. There were steep hills, which contained caves, rising above the creek. To me, a child who wanted there to exist forests and wilderness, this small park was salvation.

And there were trails running along the ridge of the hills which we called the Monkey Trails. The Butterfly Boy lived on the edge of the Monkey Trails and we often encountered him when we were playing. He was a boy with ears you could see through and he carried a butterfly net.

We heard the trains at night. We imagined that tramps rode the trains. Our parents told us to stay away from the tracks. It was like staying away from the gravel pit.

The difference between a tramp and me was that I had my four bedroom walls, I had never hitched a ride on anything. My hands sweated too much. I could feel my palms as the door compartments flashed by at speeds of thirty to sixty miles per hour and it would be the same as standing with a jump rope at recess and trying to jump in.

We played all over the Monkey Trails making houses and forts and conducting raids. At the bottom was the suspicious looking brown creek. Near the top were houses and especially the large brick one where the Butterfly Boy lived.

I once visited his collection. His collections were beautiful, each labelled and spiked through the "heart" (I assumed) of the butterfly. We must have made few admiring remarks but at the time we were just too dumb to appreciate the Butterfly Boy.

≥   ≥   ≥

Tramps, we thought, could be foreign. They could not be married. If they were women, they must be bearded. But they were not women. It was possible to become like a tramp and go roving and live in one set of clothes. And it was possible to play, as we did, on the Trails, making houses and sweeping them clean and setting up tables and chairs. We always used rusted tin cans with the dirt knocked out as groceries. We liked to make brooms. We thought there should be a stockade fence. There were many arrivals and departures. There was more to do on the Monkey Trails, in a single afternoon or morning, than anywhere. We exchanged friendship, there being sometimes four to six of us. In the alliances put together, we hoped always to find an arrangement that lasted at least three to four days.

We played in sewer pipes and thought they were great. We never felt hunger, had to forget hunger like we forgot having to pee. Whatever we needed the woods could provide. If it were a lamp, well then, we used lacy tin cans. If it were armies or wars or treaties, we had our allies which changed with each new day. Even our occupations varied.

≥   ≥   ≥

Sometimes in our town somebody would turn up missing and the police cars would be out and it would be suspected that the person had been killed or kidnapped. One day it happened that a child was lost. We, of course, ran to the Monkey Trails even though we didn't know for certain what side of town was involved, but a missing child was a serious thing, and we should even go across the creek, looking.

The water in the creek was poison. It was yellowish and we thought that if you put your hands into it to situate a log, your hands might get contaminated. (We used words like that back then). And although the water looked shallow it actually was deep. I had grandparents who owned a cottage on a lake and I learned to wade out in the lake and know where it turned to a deeper bottom. I had spent a good deal of my life looking at my legs under water so I knew about the deception of water, how it could be deeper than you think. Besides, the thing about our creek was this: we thought it was quicksand.

We had all seen movies about people disappearing in the jungles after a plane crash. In the movies, the person waded into a creek of quicksand and just as his mouth was buried by the sand it hit bottom and the action of the quicksand suddenly, miraculously, stopped. But sometimes it didn't. That's why none of us ever went over to the other side.

But when someone has been murdered–has been missing all night–it is necessary to take chances and it is out of the question to leave the other side of the woods unsearched just because the water is quicksand or there is no bridge–even if your parents told you not to.

We could always find some pieces of lumber or a log lying around to make a bridge. Occasionally we would find one that somebody else put there. It gave us a queer feeling to think the woods were played in by anyone else. These must be our woods, empty before we came and empty after we left. But people had been there, and I couldn't say who or how because, other than the Butterfly Boy, we never saw anyone.

On this particular day there was already a log forming a bridge. We had a neighbor named Lanny with us and he was oldest so he went over first. I was in clothes that didn't hitch up very well, holding my feet off the water to save my shoes and straddling the log. I put my hands in front and back and inched along. I was all legs like a spider conquering the creek, but at last I arrived and brushed myself off and headed for the adventure. Sarah Jane came after me. She was skinny and skittish sometimes.

The woods over there was really different. There was more open space. The trails were tame. You could even see houses and if you could see houses that meant there was no wilderness there at all. Even the bugs were boring–there were none of those bubble bugs on scum, none of those water tension bugs that eternally skate across the skin of the surface making kissing-sounding popper noises through their mouths.

And so we all went back to the other side, Lanny left us and went home and that's when the tramp appeared. He did not seem to want anything. He seemed to be dawdling. He looked at the ground.

Then he suddenly looked up, turned to us as if to offer something. "Have you ever seen that?" he said. Something like that.

I couldn't understand him. I didn't know what he said.

"..."

Or did he say?

But I know for sure the next thing he did I saw he had reached inside his pants.

Now Sarah Jane was sometimes day dreaming and she did not notice what had just happened. She still had the gentle, intelligent and open look she always got when we were on an adventure. I knew I was going to have to inform her of danger.

I shouted to Sarah Jane, "Run! Hurry up! Run!"

We ran out of the woods and he didn't try to follow us. We didn't speak and we just kept looking back and walking fast until we were among all the houses of the neighborhood and then we began to think about what we might tell our parents.

At dinner that night I told my parents that I had crossed the creek and they threatened me by saying I could have drowned. In my family, drowning was a painful word. I was ashamed that I had caused them to concern themselves again with the word.

I did not tell about the man easily but I knew Sarah Jane was telling and I couldn't be considered to have held something back. I really didn't have the words to say it–wouldn't have known to say 'exposed himself'. Just as I thought, my parents were angry about it.

Angry at me. I could have been killed. I had no business fooling around that way. And, somehow, I felt it would have been better not to have mentioned the man.

Not to have crossed the creek would have been impossible and not trying to find the lost child, impossible too, and this ending they were suggesting in which I died was especially impossible: a blot where I sank from life leaving them orphans of me. The next day we read in the papers that the missing child had been found, on the other side of Lansing.

ða.   ða.   ða.

The kids that summer, the big kids, kept on parking on the sand road by the Monkey Trials, at night when we were in bed, and it was at night that the tramps came, got off the trains, lighted their fires and cooked their cans. I never really caught on that it was not really the tramps that one ought to be afraid of, that it was something else, maybe our worse selves.

It was near the Monkey Trails that one more incident occurred. Some teenagers 'parked', a boy and a girl, and left the motor running and were asphyxiated. When the police came and found them we heard that their bodies were stuck together!

Sometime over the next weeks and months, we stopped going to the Monkey Trails or following the creek home from school. Nothing to match that time came to take its place. We tried to make our height, looks, even the way we walked, acceptable. We wore matching sweaters, or letterman's jackets and we did not tell anyone, at home, anything.

An Autobiographical Fragment

I had a good grandma and a naughty grandma and they both lived on lakes and they each had cocker spaniels—one named Corky who was blond and one named Barkus who was black. The grandfather who was married to the naughty grandma never swore, the other one often did. One never drank, the other drank. One worked at General Motors and sang tenor to Silent Night and that is the grandfather who was such a great appreciator of the "event." When I became a member of Westminster Presbyterian Church, he inscribed my Bible with my full name in aquarium blue ink, possibly so I would know what a serious thing I had done. He, himself, was the 169th member. He urged me to join something called the Rainbow Girls where there was a lot of processing and formality. He was a Mason.

Since he worked for General Motors, he bought a new Oldsmobile every year. Usually the color was white or robin's-egg-blue. Then when he paid us a visit he parked in the driveway so we could see his new egg-glossed car. He was waiting for the moment he could show us how the windows whined. We had old cars. One of our cars had a hole straight through the floor, so we were impressed. This grandfather kept a record of accomplishments and events in a series of small, leather log books.

6 April: Left Lansing 10 a.m.–mother and I (and Corky)–came via Hastings. All roads okay & trip uneventful. Stopped in Delton for a few groc. & oleo. Everything Okay at cottage & had plumbing connect. & pump going in about 30 min. Saw oil man & had barrel filled. House heated Okay & we were very comfortable. Swept, mopped, put up screens & when house was in order we finished digging out the stump & tipped it over in hole & covered it up. Took rotted rail boards off the sail boat and will replace them. Today is Corky's birthday, & no cake.

Corky was the blond cocker spaniel. I had seen my grandfather get him to race around the living room after a rubber toy with a bell inside. Panting and snapping, Corky used to leap into the air while his toenails raked up the rug. The whole business was not permitted by my grandmother and usually ended a little after it should have.

That was in the city. At the lake, Corky was allowed to run and go without a chain or leash and live like a real dog. My grandfather always kept control over him though. He called him in a very paternal way–Cork! And he had a whistle which only the dog could hear.

Also, it seemed as if we had no weather in town. But at the Lake you could tell it was going to rain by signs in the sky. You could watch the rain come across the lake. If the weather were windy, for example, you didn't continue your day as planned. The fish didn't bite when it was windy.

My grandfather used to take the heads off the biggest fish–usually they were bass, but sometimes it might be a bullhead or catfish–and nail them on the beech trees about eye level. These fish heads stared out across from each other, astonished totems.

"That's a wide-mouthed bass," my grandfather would say accurately, staring at their mouths (filled now with cobwebs). The eyes lost flesh more slowly and particles clung like museum mummies. By keeping these heads, he felt able to point to any fish he had caught. So we had rows of them, the stretched open mouths still hungering for air.

He marked the beginning of every summer with an April entry carefully dated.

29 April: Opening day. Glorious. A few boats out but the weather is cool. The trees are beautiful today.

And in the fall, he took a solemn, morbid glance back at life in town.

27 Sept: Bass hit nights only. Sunday caught nineteen bluegills on crickets. Season is almost over and we must hibernate in Lansing with our memories.

In July, 1945 he wrote:

One week of our vacation has elapsed. Went to Kazo [Kalamazoo] 1 day & spent another afternoon at fair at Hastings which was punk. No sailing until today but LOADS of large bluegills. Got them 30 ft. down on crickets. Lake receding fast. Put out 20 ft. more of dock this week. Front yard all sand & dug up ready for black dirt for lawn. Expect to go home Mond. to install new water heater & go to Ionia Fair Tues. then back here Wed. for bal. of 3 weeks of vacation. Looks like I am thru at Fisher-Lansing as far as production is concerned [during the War, the Fisher Body Plant in Lansing produced fighter planes]. What next? Will find out tomorrow p.m. I hope.

8 Aug: Big bluegills started biting about Aug. 1, but the real RUN started Sat. Wind in north and oodles of boats collected along channel near north shore from line opposite point. Biting crickets in 35 ft. water. Fishing best in afternoon & evening. Stop biting soon after sun goes down behind trees.

My grandfather and grandmother left the cottage in the fall as late as they could and I noticed they sometimes took several final goodbyes.

21 October: Leaves falling fast. Dark with cool east wind. 7:30 and we are about to depart.

29 October: A BEAUTIFUL day–sunshine, temperature about 75. Breeze off the lake from southwest.

30 Nov: darn cold–but beautiful 20 degrees in cottage–covering things & taking screens in.

It was characteristic of my grandfather to begin preparing for an event, thoroughly, as soon as he saw it ahead. He started talking about his retirement from Fisher Body when he was in his fifties. He retired, in word and thought, at least every single year after. When the time actually came, perhaps he was prepared. At least, he had suffered it many times over. He had gathered a huge collection of neckties and dress shirts and bedroom slippers for a man whose parents had been unsteady, a person, people feared, who would never find himself. To me, the very idea that he could ever have been viewed as not making a success was hilarious. My mother told me that people used to wonder if H. George Newth would ever get himself together. First he was a barber, then he was a clerk, then he went to evening school. He changed jobs so many times people could not keep up. He met my grandma when he was eighteen and she was only fifteen, secured his job at the Fisher Body plant and worked there for the rest of his life, long enough to be senior to everyone.

I respected his practical way with life and usually took care not to reveal my own, though I did uncover the tip of my thoughts to him sometimes, and I believe he took pleasure in my perverse reversals. A running debate between us was whether the worms felt the hook. He would have voted Republican.

In the last of the log books, the cottage, the well, the cleared land, seems to fail him. Still, he writes down information he hopes to pass on.

–sunk cream can near maple–to locate joint, or cream can, dig 3 ft. east of trees as shown–if tile plugs again we should make dry well out of cement blocks south from joint west.

–Ernie Shed 68 F2 Crooked Lane–fixes stoves.

Among the lures in his tackle box, his favorite, the one that nobody else used, was his wooden bass lure. The paint on it was blistered, and there were shiny hooks, and two wise, comprehending eyes. This lure was painted white and red, and it worked better than the ones with rainbow-colored scales, and better than the silver-fish. He always said it worked better than anything you could buy.

I wasn't told about his death on the day it occurred. By that time, I was a Freshman in college. It happened early in the morning, I guess, before breakfast. He hadn't been doing anything–for years he occupied himself making Christmas ornaments–so maybe he was still asleep. What he had been doing for a long time was try to stay alive, and he tried much longer and harder than I would have. When I heard the news, I couldn't shake the thought that, all that same day and some of the day before, I had been living "out of synch."

My grandmother gave the bass lure to my father. It still had some of the red paint on it. There was its broad bug face and its skirt of double hooks suggesting a large insect or frog which moves quietly over the surface. In the water, it made faint movements and ripples, or gave the silhouette of a quiet swimmer. I had seen it so many times animated by my grandfather. Like Corky, it never seemed to belong to anyone else.

You could eat off her floors, you could eat off my grandmother's walls, any walls, you could eat off her blinds, her shower curtains, her front porch, you could have eaten anywhere in her house and not have found it dirty or dusty or unclean. I remember my grandmother used to list what she had cleaned that day. Blinds, Venetian blinds–one hour and a half, washed and dried. Kitchen floor, washed and waxed. Dusted living room and bedroom.

My grandmother had a smooth, plate-like beauty but she was not aware of how she looked. She was small and well proportioned and wore lots of rings. She had one with a Tiffany setting holding a pink stone the color of a rabbit's eye. She also wore a ring from her club (senior to the Rainbow Girls), and her wedding rings, wire thin. As her hands got more arthritic and the knuckles swelled, she transferred some of her rings out to the little fingers, and added bracelets.

She had a rosebud mouth and small, perfect teeth that were edged, like a garden, with gold. And all in back of her front teeth was a wondrous gold ridge. She used to make a little sucking sound with her mouth as she talked.

"Hell (two syllables) oh" (lower tone) she said when she answered the phone. Her phone was on a glass-topped desk and it was ivory and she cleaned it and kept it polished. She kept the desk polished and she had everything in it–a pad and a small pencil on top. The cord of the phone stretched lazily when she took up the arm of the phone and spoke into it. "Hello," she said like she was sure who she was. Who were you? She said hello like someone who had hold of an ivory phone and was standing by a desk with a glass top. Then she put the phone back in its cradle the way a receptionist puts you in a blank space in a leather book.

"Huuuun eee" she called me. No matter how commanding her voice, I knew I would be accepted because I was related. Every day she had a new list of surfaces she had cleaned and while she told you, you could think what you were going to tell her, so there were never any lapses in the conversation and that was a relief.

The height of security for me was the green plastic coinholder she hung in her car on one of the knobs. She put nickels in it for parking meters. She put one in, she explained to me, whenever she had extra. There were Kleenex holders in her car too and the windows were tinted and the rugs had plastic covers over them.

My grandmother had formidable talents. She could make people feel small and stupid. Once when we were on the porch of the cottage after having gone to pick huckleberries, a car came rolling in up the hill and a lady got out that my grandmother knew. She invited us to visit her cottage which was on the other side of the lake. But the interesting thing was that my grandmother directed the conversation much as you would step on a dog's leash to hold it. My grandmother spoke warmly to her but her voice carried a warning. I could not imagine what the warning was or even how exactly it was achieved but it came from somewhere.

My grandmother folded her pretty pink lips and rolled her green almond eyes and said, "We're busy doing all our forenoon work."

We would not go.

"Oh, but I'd love you to see our house and sit on the porch with us and look at the lake," the woman chatted happily.

I tried to imagine my grandmother sitting on someone's porch not her own.

"... hmmm," said my grandma. "Your porch is very nice I am sure. But, you don't need anybody coming over to mess it up. Why don't you you come visit ours sometime."

Suddenly the invitation was turned around so that we had asked the lady to visit us. Only it had been diluted somehow so that no definite day had been set and no time. Then the woman was confused as she was about to accept by the casualness of our invitation and the lack of a place to hold on to it anywhere. She didn't know if she should come to visit us or not. All she could do was walk back uphill to her car.

I was safe with my grandmother. That was her fatal charm. She could do anything to me. I wanted to get in good with her. But I never could. She used to ask me, "Does your mother still have that china dog I gave her? No?"

Should I tell the truth or tell half, or go for the out-right lie?

"It has been left out?" my grandmother wondered, meaning outdoors. Well, she didn't do things that way. "Has it got broken?"

Meanwhile I remembered that my mother also did not like my grandmother to give her things. The china dog was probably in our basement.

My mother would not keep a plant. It would die. She would not keep knickknacks and my grandmother loved them. I could not remember when my mother cleaned things. Certainly she never made a list. She hated real silver, antiques, doilies, glass on desks and bureaus, pencil and pad sets, napkins and napkin holders, coasters for glasses in summertime (all these my grandmother gave her). She hated the frosted, prism-glass name plates for table settings, she hated vases, she hated "grandmother bracelets" and earrings and rings–they made her neck and hands feel hot. She hated sweaters and sweater holders and chains, she hated gadgets like the nickel holder and the Kleenex holder and the toilet paper cover and the rings that hang on shades and shades themselves. She hated Venetian blinds with a passion. She hated umbrella stands and mirrors and things for a bath. She hated plastic refrigerator containers and the people who tried to foist them on her, she hated family breakfasts and talking and peace and order and all those things my grandmother gave her, or did, or stood for.

Grandmother quizzed me about things she had given my mother, things long-lived because she never really gave them up. You don't have that anymore? Then she made the sucking sound with her gold and enamel teeth.

Once, at the grocery up the street, my grandmother bought a dozen eggs in a square carton, and carefully considered her list, tapped with her neat polished fingernails the carton, and she made everything she held or wore or set her eyes on even, her own–while the check-out lady with the floppy bare arms and the sweating face and untidy hair at the cash register didn't even matter, wasn't even as present as a cabbage sitting innocently nearby.

And then we walked home. We walked home to 'home' the only possible one that waited for us, on a sidewalk. We spoke to people on the way who watched and envied and it never entered my grandmother's mind that this might not be the right and only way, that the eggs we carried might not have been laid for our souls' sakes.

ॐ   ॐ   ॐ

I sat in the back. We had been riding for a long time. It was winter and the heat did not reach to the back seat. Also, there was a draft around the left window where my father was smoking and that made it cold. I sat next to my brother Donny, four years younger, who was being very quiet in the dark. Perhaps he was sleeping. I looked at my father's head. It was tall and narrow with a bony jaw and forehead. He had a swarthy skin like an Indian's and when he lighted one of his cigarettes the match lighted up the inside of his hand. At first I smelled the good smell of the match when it caught. Smoke circled overhead and then turned and went out the vent. Then the smell was no good.

We were going to Detroit. We still had a long way to go, how much farther I didn't dare to ask. I turned to look at my mother. I saw her soft features, the almost babyish face in its softness, its youth, the lightest brown curling hair, the soft cheeks and the neck and shoulders.

It was too warm up there in front and my mother had put off her coat and laid it over her shoulders not bothering to pull it around her. My mother and father looked so young. (I was all of eleven at the time). It almost seemed they were not old enough to know where they were going.

They stopped at a farm house and again at a gas station to put water into the radiator. Unlike my grandpa's car, this car had all kinds of things wrong with it. We had so far to go and the pavement seemed so hard, it made my teeth jar. So much pavement to cross on those tires that weren't any good! So much pavement to stretch this old, full-of-smoke car over that carried my brother and me and my parents who looked so young and inexperienced.

My father held the cigarette up near the second joint so he could clasp the steering wheel and not be bothered by the cigarette in his hand. It was the mark of an experienced smoker. Now he revolved it down his hand the way they do in the circus trick with the small, juggling balls. The cigarette suddenly extended out from the tip of his hand and the finger went "pok" and the ash fell neatly. Then the cigarette was back near the second joint. My father did this over and over. In between times, he checked the radio stations.

My mother was giving my father a tongue lashing. It was going on and on. My mother's soft mouth that the front teeth protruded from–she needed her teeth straightened–bit down hard on the black bitter words of her anger. At last my father said, softly, "That's enough."

Suddenly we were in trouble. The car wobbled. My father braked. Instantly we were silent in the dark and alone. Other cars whizzed past us. My father got out, his thin, weary body cradling this new worry like a flame. He made us get out. My brother woke up and looked forward, wide-eyed, while we waited there on the highway.

Then, in one horrible second, the car slid off the jack. I could almost feel the lurch of the car and the slippery, uncontrolled movement as if my stomach poured up its contents. My mother had been staring at the back windows. Now, the movement of the car off the jack made her body jiggle–just once.

It reminded me of the time she had asked to bring my younger brother, Doug, home with us. He was two and he had drowned. She wanted to bring Doug home for the last time. She had slumped just that way and I had looked at her from the back seat the whole way home. My mother had asked to bring him in the car and she had slumped against the door in the front seat and I had been petrified of the idea of bringing him in the car, and I said, "No." I was also afraid for my mother, that she might fall out. And perhaps I thought that she would want to fall out. I could see why she would want to bring him with her and why she sobbed and sobbed while my father got more and more stern.

In the end, the ambulance took care of him and I told my mother they would take care of him (if it really was my brother anymore, which I doubted now that he had gone to heaven) but I partially understood that my mother felt it was still her responsibility to take him home with us in the car. After all, he was only two and a baby. It was up to God to take care of him and all the angels in heaven would be singing around him, but still, we had his blanket down here with us.

There was a terrific crash. I stopped thinking. Had the car fallen on my father who was underneath? But there was my father alive and reflected in the lights in the windows. He was getting in. The car had not fallen on him when it slipped. He was so skinny he had not been caught under the car.

We rode on again. My mother looked towards my father and I did also from the back. My mother looked soft and young and my father looked thin. Bony, his face and his pointed cheekbones and his knuckled hands that held things. My father wanted to protect, to care for things, I knew from the way his hands looked on the steering wheel. And he had had a child cut from his flesh and he was like a flame that was flickering. No one said anything.

ea   ea   ea

My father was looking for something in the music. His fingers seemed to search first here, then there, jumping from one combination to another. Sometimes he got it. Then his eyes would grow wide and his cheeks inflate. "Oh baby."

He had played the saxophone since he was ten. He didn't care if he were popular in school as I did. He wore a cape, when a cape was called for, in the marching band. I know because I have a picture and he looks rather strange. A diagonal strap goes from his chest to the sax.

With the mouth piece in his mouth he couldn't talk. I had to watch his fingers jump, or his eyes in order to guess what he was thinking. No one would know I was his daughter when he was playing the sax because he was in another world. One thing about the Newth side was that they were musicians.

I understood what being in another world meant though if it was like opening a closet that held winter coats, and meeting yourself face to face in the mirror on the door, or, you opened the glass-front bookcase to wedge out that book beside the Bible and heard the noise the grownup people made and settled in the soft, velvety chair hooked with pins that held doilies and looked at the books, turned the pages, while Corky slept in his wealth of blond curls in a pose of running, Sundays, at Grandma's. And then I took out the difficult set of toy plastic men with joints that would take arms where the legs should be and heads where the arms would be and there were never enough pieces to fully conceive the dream I wanted to make.

My father played like Tommy Dorsey in dance bands. He could play anything. I remember the silver slide instrument that was so cold and the combs that buzzed your lips, the ukelele that you could never get the pick out of (put in storage in the attic with the *Life* magazines that got to be too loud about the war).

There was a flugel horn and the puffed pipes of plastic. What were they called? They sat on the piano like all knickknacks of life which some people treasured (in the Newth family each member owned one, except my grandmother, of course) and the trumpet. The saxophone was a gleaming sensuous lady. The slide horn? But there was something that was the name of a kind of fruit. Was it called the lemon lime? ....Ah, the "sweet potato": it was THAT, after all.

❧   ❧   ❧

We always went to the cottage at Wall Lake in the summers and the previous summer we were there as always every weekend. My grandfather's career had taken him into the upper echelons while my grandmother's corresponding eighth grade education led her to an uncomprehending distrust of General Motors' stocks, the so-called GM Stocks that she didn't think could be relied on. But my grandfather had purchased land and had built a cottage.

To my surprise one weekend along about the end of summer, my grandmother and grandfather left us alone to enjoy ourselves. We were my mother and father, my brother, Don who was six, and my two-year-old brother Doug. I am absolutely convinced my grandmother and grandfather didn't believe we could handle closing up the cottage.

It got cold immediately after they left, but we took a boat ride in the speed boat, the three of us children under the bow where we could feel every slam of the waves.

Then after lunch I lay down on the sofa to read and think. I was ten, I did most of my cogitating during nap time or quiet time. On this day, I remember that my mother was vacuuming and my father and Doug were outdoors working in the yard. Later we couldn't find Doug and my mother sent my brother Don and me to look for him near the store to see if he had wandered up there. We were kept up there for what seemed hours. I remember somebody bought us an orange drink and he drank his but I wouldn't. Finally, someone even took us to their home. At last, our father came to get us. I understood that the emergency teams were trying to resusitate my brother because he had fallen into the water, the very shallow water at the edge of the lake. And no one had heard him if he cried because it was so windy.

Our father said, "Doug's all right. He is home with us."

But I saw his face and I distrusted him.

We plodded home, unspeaking, and went into the cottage and upstairs where our mother was and she held out her arms to us and said, "Help me."

So we knew for sure that Doug had died.

I didn't go down to the water's edge but I could imagine the place where he drowned. I wandered around, looked at the shady side of the cottage, waited for my parents to pack and load the car, saw Judy Hyde, a girl I played with, all bloody from itching her bites, her whole body pricked with red scabs, and her mother pale and dark, leaning against a clothes line, and crying for us.

The newspaper summed up our tragedy in one inch: Douglas John N—two years, dead of drowning. Berry County, Michigan.

A man at the lake put a rope in his dog's mouth and turned in a circle until the dog's feet left the ground. But the dog wouldn't let go of the rope until finally he was hanging on with just his teeth. And that's how I felt.

The Puff Ball

My great-grandfather says, thinking out loud, "Don't look now, but there's someone in the yard. The boy is skinny too. Dressed in a pair of grey pants and a white shirt. He's on his lunch break or som'en like that. Who's that?"

My great-grandfather didn't know it was William, his grandson, who had come to visit him on his lunch break.

"The boy's slamming the car door and checking on somethin' near the ground. Digging in his right pocket in front and left pocket. Coming up the walk."

"The dog, shaking himself, always likes company. Missy will nose him out.

The dog wades into the new-found sunshine.

"Who is that?" my great-grandfather says again. "Looks like a snail or a cloud swirl or a storm over there. Must be rain this afternoon."

"This is something, I don't know him. Why, he is coming up here."

The boy, my father, stands behind the door.

The dog scrapes his paws one by one onto the screen. The boy/man now peers inside, the dog caroling.

"Hi, Granddad. It's me. William."

"Come on in." This would be something. I didn't know him. My own grandson!

William watches Missy wash herself, wet the loose rags of her belly. She bites at something near her tail.

"Gosh, you took me by surprise." Granddad offers William a chair. Shakes the dust out of this cushion. "My grandson. Well."

William looks out of the corner of his eye at the landscape that he can see out the windows of the old farm. He sees the hedges laid out in squares set off by fences made of tree roots. Couldn't get regular fences. Getting them out of the ground! The roots looked like tom cats scratching in the dirt and rolling over and clawing.

"Want to show you my gypsy moth trap," Granddad tells him. "but first —"

He brings his grandson into the front room where a big woman is sitting by the window.

"I braid Grandma's hair every morning and I get her dressed and fix her all up good,–Don't I Grandma?–And, I comb her hair all nice and do up the dishes. I probably don't do it as good as you would like. I'm a man."

"I do the best I can. I don't feel too well either. Do I, Grandma?" She smiles.

Every so often, she worries that he is telling lies.

"Arthur?" she says anxiously. "What are you saying?"

He grins. "I fix her up pretty good, and do dishes!"

"Yes," says Grandma chewing on her loose lips. "Arthur does all the dishes."

"Sometimes, I don't know, she can't even get up on her feet at all to get to the bathroom. She's real poorly and I don't know how long I can hang on." He says this just to William, softly.

"We do all right, though, don't we, Grandma? It's hard on an old man. I'll be eighty-four next June."

"Arthur, what are you telling him?"

"Oh, just telling him how you and I fight all the time!"

❧   ❧   ❧

My father had turned on Stine Road, gone past Uncle Victor's new lime green ranch. Didn't have time to stop though. Deer on the lawn, high up as dust on the road, driving the car through the country with sun shining and doing something I ought, he was thinking, going to visit Granddad.

Granddad's house is set in from the road. His big oak opposite looks ready to split. Grass hasn't been mowed. Hope the tires don't hit. Park beside the mailbox. In the sand, rocks have worked to the surface. Gosh, it's hot. The path to his door overgrown and two side windows patched with tape.

Knock.

He isn't around. Blue jay springs out. Within, muffled, a dog barks.

Here he comes. Through the glass of the porch door, I can almost see him but the glass is pretty gray.

Doesn't know me at first? This is something.

"Hi, Granddad. Here I am. Yes," and my hand reaches.

He looks pleased. He knows me and he is so surprised. Granddad is still the same. Lighter eyes, whiter skin. He's hunched over, caved-in, and it looks like there is a rock on his back under the shirt.

Wearing suspenders and still lots of white hair. Perspiring. Blue eyes.

We could go inside but the dog's jumping all over. I think Granddad wants to come out. Yes, he is going out.

"My dog, Missy," he says. "Down."

She is a small black and white one. Smart. Sniffs me. Doesn't know me. Granddad turns and I follow his lopsided back.

"I want to show you my gypsy moth traps."

"I want to see them too."

"It's a hundred steps." Grunt and whisper "...two ...three."

"To the mailbox, alone," he continues. His legs like twigs beside the sturdy walking stick. How many steps to the gypsy moth trap?

"I want you to see it," Grandpa says. Missy leaps near his knees and his legs crack. "I want you to see it."

We have I suppose a great distance to go. Granddad waves his hands towards the field on the left

"Sliney's land," he says. "That land." As if we were moles we clamber over the rocks in the road. My eye follows the line of telephone poles. "And over there is Taffy's house, remember."

"As a rule there would be two ruts leading clearly."

I do not see any ruts. We incline slowly rather than walk towards the base of a tree.

"It is a large maple. Here it is. Where is that thing?"

I don't see any trap.

"Isn't that odd. It must have gave way. This winter."

He stands perplexed. "It's all changed," he tells me. "The old sugar bush. I can't walk down there anymore. You go."

So I go on down there. The metal troughs for boiling the sap are caved in on jewel weed and wormy wood and mice. Leaves. Chipmunks. It's gone. Just gone. A piece of hard tool maybe. No path leading out, very little light. Nothing left of the road. Where are the horses pulling sleds? It will soon be impossible to find also.

I once had to be responsible for keeping the maple syrup fires going all night. I was there with one of Granddad's dogs. He's had a million of them. And we were sitting there dozing when Jeez I heard an owl and I jumped up so fast the gun went off and the dog and I both took off, scared. We let the fire go out. The dog scared also. It was always a spooky place.

Back I go to Grandpa's house. In his kitchen, he is by the ice box. He has told me to sit at the table and join him for lunch.

"A light lunch," he says. He takes out a knife. It is one of the old worn-handled black knives with the curved blade. He rubs his stubby thumb against it as if it itches, then turns his back to me and lights the burner. Starts splattering the fat. Goes to the top of the refrigerator. Reaches way up lopsided and takes down a small green ribbed plate that has something on it. He brings it down eye level.

"See what we've got today!" He takes it like a fortune teller's gazing ball. It is a grey-white dome.

"A puff ball! I collected it!" He turns to the board, cuts it in sure strokes, thud, and drops it zizzling.

"Don't give me much."

On the board it has fallen like white rubber. There is a sort of resin upon the outside which has hardened into a crust and little bugs harbor there. Several half formed balls, like clones, cling to the base.

He holds up a piece of the uncooked part.

"Everything has cycles," he explains "–gypsy moths and cicada, fungus good and bad. Strange. Folks say fungus comes from old rotting wormy wood. The kind you find in old lumber or trees. One old book even says puff balls are the sperm of birds."

"There are some growing near here," he goes on, "and I have heard they grow at the Red Sea." (I have always wondered how the midwest could be made to connect with the Bible land. Now, I see this is a problem Granddad has handled).

"The book says the birds copulate with each other and puff balls develop from them spontaneously. It's a fact. But, really, they just grow near the base of decaying trees." He thumbs a flap. It looks like an umbilical cord of the meat. There are sub-sections of a consistency of mud, white or mottled with yellow.

I shake my head.

I can't eat it after all.

He is sorry. I am missing something.

The puff ball sits in light grease. I eat some crackers with him, slowly, till he has eaten most and then I stop and stare out of the window.

He says he will make coffee I say no. Swirls of fruit flies hover over the lid when he opens the pot.

I must get back to my work.

"Goodbye, Granddad."

Missy comes in, just then. Panting. He reaches for her. His eyes have clouds in them. I shake his hand and make the clouds part for tears.

"Goodbye."

Like all old people he says goodbye as if forever. I wish he would will me his arrowheads. I walk toward my car. I notice the peanut shaped treads made of sand. I get in. Perfectly formed peanuts, lying there, made by my car's tires, some broken in two, some perfect.

A puff ball! Out of decaying matter, well, I'll be damned. Long ago people ate them and called them bread but not me, a person that likes plain food. I almost get sick thinking about it.

A Good
Winter Coat

It is still perfectly true that the weather in places like Nebraska and the Northern Great Plains is radical and inhuman. My other grandmother, Grandma Messenger, was from Kansas and when she moved to Fair Haven, Michigan, it must have seemed like coming East. She reported that in Kansas the temperature got so high she showered and then dripped dry to the mail box. But in Michigan the weather could be fiercely changeable, subject to floods, drought, below freezing and as much as one hundred feet of snow coming off the Great Lakes.

Her house at Fair Haven was full of antiques. The house had a stairway which divided and became two separate stairs that went up on the right and the left into a balcony over second-story windows. The trees were mature. I could see the seawall and the freighters. This was not a little lake. It was Lake St. Clair, almost one of the Great Lakes.

When we came for Thanksgiving, it was always dark inside except for one slice of light coming in eyebrow windows and my grandmother, like Eleanor Roosevelt, sat at the window waiting for us.

We could see straight through the house to Lake St. Clair moving and stirring in the back window. And Barkus, the black cocker spaniel, ran back and forth and shoved his head between my legs. I used to begin playing hide and seek right away, so he couldn't sniff me. Or I went to the bathroom where I thought about nature. I was greatly fond of nature, and of thinking, and of the two going together.

Then I'd go upstairs to my bedroom and fool with the suitcase. I had a room at the top of the stairs on the landing. It had an antique bed and dresser. I would look deep in the mirror for some glimpse of what was to come: Guinevere, Snow white, a witch, someone living in a log, someone trapped in a rolling pen.

In the morning I would get up early. The new day. Where was my prince? There were the barges and the boats. Something moved against the smudge of horizon. Canada. I opened the door to the dining room which was at the foot of the stairs and there my grandmother was pulling bloody strings out of a turkey with long crooked fingers.

A knocking would grow louder. It was accompanied by chokes and a phlegm-filled cough. It went on and on, rising to a landslide of throat and lungs and chest. And he threw open the door. Grandfather.

He had taken a shower and he was nude to the waist. I could see his stomach and the army belt and khaki pants. His chest was covered with fat. He looked at me and I was terrified. He coughed then and laughed and laughed on and on until he was gasping. At the same time, he smacked himself on the chest like Tarzan.

"Where's my breakfast?"

It didn't seem quite right the way Grandfather hugged everybody all the time. It was not as if he used to do it. Years ago, he wouldn't even look at anybody. But, suddenly, he was like the cocker spaniel jumping up on people when they came for a visit. And the dog, the real cocker spaniel, was bad enough groping all around a person and my new winter coat getting covered with dog hairs. He had changed since his heart attack.

My grandmother Messenger was not going to go to church this Thanksgiving because the turkey needed her. But Grandfather was going. So was my mother, whose light brown hair curled and whose face was soft and powdered and who wore something pretty so that my father would try to kiss her.

Father wore a thin, rumpled shirt and just as we were ready, Mother saw what he was wearing and said, "You're not wearing that."

"Well," (sheepishly).

Anger. Undiluted, turn-around anger suddenly everywhere, my father trying to nose it into a corner with a smile. But he had been outdoors starting up the car and he was shivering. Powdery air came from his mouth and his face looked blotchy even under the soft felt hat. So he slipped away going back to the car. It was a Studebaker, exactly the same on the front as on the back and the doors opened backwards so that if you were moving they would rip off. It was Grandpa's car and it smelled of Grandpa.

Tears rolled down my father's face as he scraped the windshield with his bare hands. He clapped his chapped hands on his knees. He was stooped over. He smoked. He was skinny and I remembered that he would die before I ever grew up, as my other grandmother told me. That's what would happen.

But the rest of us must go to church. I got into the Studebaker next to my brother who was looking at his dirty hands and his long gruesome fingernails. I wore gloves. Inside them, my ring pushed into the skin. The gloves were white and the sky was white and blue and the canals were green on the way to church this morning.

All the way to church my grandpa hummed. His monotonous humming of no tune at all was a signal he was near–either at work in the garage scraping down furniture or puttering in his study pecking out one of the business letters that began:

"Yours of the first instance received in hand and contents noted."

He once wrote to his family:

"Dear all eight of you, It might be well to give you more information about our finances, so that you need not be concerned about us and, if it becomes necessary for us to spend less on presents and to curtail trips to visit you, you will know that it applies to all alike."

As a boy in Missouri he started up his own grocery delivery business. A newspaper article said that "he was not out for the fun of the thing but for business." That was like him. Over his favorite chair in the living room was the picture of Aunt Vonette with her finger propping her head and the curl in the middle of her forehead. And above that was a cold air register which went right up into my bedroom.

"A man called today," I heard Grandma say to him one night. "He said he wanted to know if you were going to meet with the Republicans."

Grandfather took in a noisy breath.

"You've turned Republican?" she asked him.

"Sometimes we have to do these things," he countered, almost contentedly.

From above, I saw him turn his bald head.

". . . for business," he added.

"For business?" Grandma said.

He laughed.

"Mother," he said.

"I think that is really turning," Grandma said. She was out of sight now.

"Yes, so I can keep with the right people, so I can keep my job."

Grandpa had been an engineer until the Depression. Now he sold signs from home. He typed with two fingers letters on business stationery that said Messenger Sign Service.

When Vonette got married, Grandpa had a heart attack just before the wedding. He almost couldn't walk down the aisle because his feet grew huge blisters.

Now he knew they would have to sell Fair Haven because the window screens were heavy and Grandma had to lean out of the windows to put them in. And mowing was a problem. Vonette mowed the grass wearing shorts and men's shirts and came in with fish flies covering her legs and moccasins and hair. Afterwards, a few of them even would attach themselves to the underside of the horsehair furniture. Fish flies were the May Flies that spawned in large numbers around lakes. They stuck to everything. They would coat the surface of the water when we went swimming and it was hard not to swallow them.

A peacock farm could be seen from the front windows and sometimes at lunch, I would hear the cries. I was aware of them at night too–a mysterious squalling. Mother complained, "They sound like crying babies."

And next door was a vacant house. The lawn was all grown-over and contained immense tiger lilies tall as a grown-up and broken walks and weeds. A boy whose family was renting over there tried to make me kiss him. He claimed I would marry him.

"I'm going into the navy and you're going to marry me," he said. "I know!"

He didn't know. I ran from him, because the thought of falling prey to this mean, sneaky horrible person was too much for me, clear around the house, passing the glittering lake the first time, and hoping that my mother or grandmother would hear, passing the flowers near the house and the house and all the familiar places in a dizzy circle I ran and still he chased me. I was winded but again I passed the lake. Again. "I'm going to kiss you!" he screamed.

        ᔰ   ᔰ   ᔰ

The house at Fair Haven had a black wrought-iron fence that was curved in tracings and curlicues of what seemed to me a heavenly language. Anchor Bay, Marine City, New Baltimore. Some of the homes had wooden picket fences but many were iron with twisted spikes and some had wooden balls on top and some were wire and wiggly, and it was a joy beyond telling to follow one fence after another as they joined in these different languages. I would be riding in the back seat of our car and trying to be first to see the lake behind the houses, to distinguish the lake from the sky, the way it glittered, sank and rose, the image it presented, so unlike land.

When I walked over the footbridge with Grandma to get the mail at the post office, I was able to see the lake through vents in the road, lapping beneath, strangely alive.

"Years ago," it seemed to say ...slap "before you were born" ...slap! It echoed and was yellow. I was on top of it and yet, I feared it.

SLAP! it said as I took myself over it with Grandmother.

        ᔰ   ᔰ   ᔰ

When we arrived at Fair Haven, Grandmother would be sitting at the front windows in a wicker chair. She crossed one leg over the other and kept a hand on Barkus. If it were morning, long shadows would be coming from the hedges that went all around the fenced-in yard where the birds flew to the bird bath. If Grandma let Barkus out in winter he would churn up a swirl of snow and scare them.

She always woke early and stepped into the day without rearranging it. Later, Mother, with small sad eyes, would come down to sit with her and together they drank coffee. They didn't even want anyone else to get up. My brother and I had to promise to stay in bed. When we did get up, Grandmother gave us each rolls for breakfast. Then we said, "Why are your fingers crooked that way? Do you have broken bones in your fingers?"

        ᔰ   ᔰ   ᔰ

Now when I am grown and married, if I were able to come back, would I see the fences beginning and the large summer houses and the flags and behind them a mark that is the beginning of the lake. New Baltimore, Marine City, Anchor Bay, Fair Haven and then, the house itself with a sagging front porch and dormers, the tiger lilies, fierce flames speckled with orange shooting up bells on them, and the dark peonies, crawling with ants. In the back would I find the garage where Grandfather refinished furniture, smelling of sawdust and sea?

❧   ❧   ❧

Grandmother held up one of her hands as if she were waving, out of the car window, like President Roosevelt. Then the knocking came again.

"Where's my breakfast?"

TOOOOOOOO LAAAAATE TOOOOO LATE, screamed the peacocks. TOOO LATE STRRRRRRRIIAAAAATE OOO-OOOOOOO.

One time I said to Grandmother, in front of other people, "Let me see you take out your teeth." That was a terrible mistake but Grandmother had only smiled. And once I had gone around with my hands on my hips and wearing the cardigan sweater with the heavy flowers crocheted on the breasts because I wanted to look like Aunt Vonette.

My brother and I took our money and spent it at the dime store. He bought an army tank but I bought a metal robin. It was red and grey and I took it out on the front walk and waited for something to crawl out of the cracks so I could feed it. What I found were many small ants. Then the bird would crush and "eat" the insect. I killed a great many of them.

"My brother is dumb," I remember I said to my grandmother, "look how he plays with that silly tank." And Grandmother had said, "That's no worse than trying to act more grownup than you are." Then I felt so bad, and I held the metal robin out of sight, down by my dress.

The name "Rebecca" meant a "noose", and what I wondered was whether I was caught in it or the people around me. I had no middle name and my last name was not spelled with a K but with an N and it was not German, it was English.

"The birds haven't discovered the water in the bird bath yet," said Grandmother, changing the subject. "I filled the bird bath this morning and they don't know it yet."

Grandma had a red ring that stood up on prongs pointing at you as if a star were holding it or an insect had hold of a seed twice its own weight.

       ❧   ❧   ❧

That Thanksgiving, Grandmother had been sitting at the windows. The sun was coming in under the porch and hovering. When everyone banged through the front door, Barkus jumped up and scratched my bare legs and, after we all were inside, Grandmother hugged my mother and kissed her. "Oh, Catherine," she breathed into her neck.

Then my mother did an awful thing. She began to cry.

I didn't know why, but I interpreted it to mean that she was unhappy, that our life was not going as it should. And, in the time that they held each other, I was afraid.

"Har," said Grandfather like a train that is coughing and laboring across a great distance. First he breathed, then he roared, then his breath caught and he coughed and nearly died.

"Harrrrrrr..." He hugged my head so hard it hurt my ear.

"Hao how ..." he said and began again.

But here we were! There were the chairs again with wooden wheels, the tables that had paws, the love-seat that looked like a green hump you could ride except that it tipped. There were the two four-footed stools, bigger than turtles. One was green with legs and the other, red. They made good tigers. You could charge them and knock them off their feet, and it was fun to lie down with one on your chest, its four legs in the air. This was the room where my brother and I pretended we were reindeer. But first, the Gladstone bag, with raised welts, clamped and snapped together must be hauled up to the bedroom and laid open to reveal exactly halves. And the boxy plaid trunk with coat hangers was heaved over to Mother's bed.

Underneath the cold air register, in a yellow circle like the coliseum, sat Grandfather's big custard-colored chair. It was plushy and had fork marks in it. No one else was allowed to sit there but Grandfather, who had to watch how much he ate or smoked or drank, listening to Tiger Baseball Games. Over his head, was a picture of a girl dressed in pink with bright blue eyes and a yellow curl hanging down the center of her forehead, one of her chubby fingers prodding her dimpled chin–Aunt Vonette.

Vonette was Mother's youngest sister. She had everything she needed to wear and didn't have to wash it each night the way they had to during the Depression. Vonette's bedroom took up the whole right side of the second floor. It had twin beds with fluffy covers. There was a slant closet painted blue and white and filled with shoes and there was a dresser with a blue and white skirt and blue ribbons, and a kidney-shaped stool. All around the mirror were white and blue ribbons. Even the light had a blue satin pull.

Aunt Vonette had the most wonderful grown up woman-sound in her knees. Every time she sat cross-legged in a chair, her knees would crack. And she wore Grandpa's shirts and tied the tails around her waist. She was thin and her bras were stiff and pointed and put a great load on her shoulders. She wore bikini bathing suits that laced. She had long blond hair which she braided and wound around her head like a Dane because actually the Messengers were Danes on Grandma's side.

When I was really young, Mother had to lift me into the big bed. It had carvings of grapes and there was a matching walnut bureau with a marble top and mirror.

"Your prince is looking for you from some place," I told it. I was not too ugly, not too pretty either. I spent alot of time alone or even in a closet that had a window. From there, I could look down from a row of musty, silk dresses to the other side of the lawn where a man named Mr. Champ was walking with his cane, or setting out his wooden boy sprinkler, or even once talking to Grandmother.

      ❧   ❧   ❧

"I got an A on my spelling and a B on my dictation and a star on my hibernating fowl," I said one day at lunch where I was finishing up some homework. They laughed.

"Well, I did," I said. They still laughed.

"How could you have hibernating fowl?" Mother asked. "How could there be?"

"On the spelling. You had to pick two words and make a cartoon of it," I said, "and I picked hibernation and fowl."

Vonette was sitting in the Queen Anne chair and she uncrossed her legs and got up.

"Did you know there are still cattle trails that can be seen from an airplane over Kansas?"

But Grandma said nothing and turned back to Mother.

On Thanksgiving Father liked a few pieces of white meat but Mother and Grandmother liked the dark and chewing on the bones. I liked white but only a little and then I did homework or drew in a coloring book or practiced piano on the tablecloth while the conversation unfolded and the dripping candles turned yellow outsides down. There was a liverish candle of all different colors and I watched it in the coffee pot. Our distorted faces gleamed back at us from the pot's curved sides.

Grandma hooked her bent index finger into the ring of her coffee cup and puckered her thin lips. Her other hand waved around as if it were waving a scarf away. My mother said I had hands like hers, hands that looked like they couldn't do ordinary housework.

So then, my brother and I decided to leave the table. Lately, all he wanted was to talk about pressure points and stunt men. In his room he sharpened his jackknife and tried to cut the hair on his arms. But now, when we sat at the table so long a time, we still wanted to go play together and so we took off our shoes and then, when we tried to slip them back on, could only find one and so we slid down under, to look, and that is what we did ...and we crawled away.

                                  ই   ই   ই

That year I had gotten a new winter coat. In Michigan we wore them from fall until mid April. This one had dark brown velvet for the lining and brown tweed on the outside. Snow settled in the velvet hood and I could turn my face in it to feel of its softness. The buttons were covered with the velvet too and the pockets were trimmed with it. I felt like someone in the fairy tales when I wore this coat and I hung it in the closet under the stairs on the first floor just outside the sun room. This was the under-the-stair closet that my brother and I used for hide'n seek.

In there we stepped on whatever lay on the floor in our effort to reach the back and not be caught. Grandma had fox fur-topped boots where the fur blew out and Grandpa had flat, helpless looking bucklers. Who can explain the joy of sweaters never to be worn, whose history is distant and future is yours to destroy? These we caught in our faces and mangled: the shoe holder with iron tiers that held the nurses shoes and the shoes with the cut-out toes–the grass cutting shoes–and the mole rubbers. And then the crackling and snapping sounds as hooks and umbrellas and canes, all, everything came falling! And to come out into daylight again, in the room next to Grandfather's chair, and look in the oval mirror and be all hot and excited.

But this once I must have laid my coat on a chair while we were eating in the dining room so Barkus got it and when I came out again it was chewed up. He had taken bites out of the soft squishy velvet hood and he had torn, also, the outer tweed fabric.

Mother when she saw it began to cry. Grandma just did nothing, did not even offer to spank the dog or repay us for the coat. Instead, she said to me, "You should have hung up your coat because Barkus, all dogs, will chew on things left down and in the way."

Then Mother held up the coat, trying to fit where the pieces should go and I knew I would not get a new one. Nothing else that weekend, not my father trying to leave a liquor bottle on the kitchen counter and Grandmother putting it back, nor the kiss between my grandmother and mother, had such an impact. There was no other coat like this one, hooded with a brown lining. Lost is lost.

Miss Gostelow: Teacher of Piano

In the course of time and the beginnings of things I ran into a person of strength, Miss Gostelow, Teacher of Piano.

My father, after checking what piano lessons cost, had deposited me with her when I was nine because it was important to him and because we had recently moved and had acquired a piano for our basement.

She took us into a warm living room furnished with drapes and heavy chairs. And in that room there was a portrait of a child, a little boy, dressed in a blue sailor suit with lace cuffs just getting ready to climb over a fence. He was from another age, I guessed, to be dressed that way, which only added to the effect on me of his delicious entrapment. He was almost life size, close enough to my own height to give me pause when I went by him on my way to the dining room; and I tried to catch his eye many a time and look into his face. His hands were limp and formless.

But it was in the dining room, right where a table would have been placed, that the Chickering sat and there Miss Gostelow wrote out my receipts in brown ink. She taught me music theory in that room, from a little card table, much to my stupefaction, at some distance from the keyboard and any auditory instruction. Instead, she gave me blue squares to place on lines and spaces, pink cardboard flats and grey sharps, all silent, everything completely visual.

And when she played, she came to the piano as one approaching an implement, sank to the bench, sank her hands even her arms, whole body, into the music and I had never seen anyone, any woman, approach work with such strength and reverence. She played with attention to something inside, and when she completed a phrase she listened to another as I imagined a horse and rider listen to each other. I'd go back out to where I lived and try to recapture what she'd showed me. But it was hard sitting down there in the cold with the basement windows and the 1947 wall calendars. The entire top of the upright had broken off when we'd moved it. My piano's wood was wildly grained, and wild was a clue to her performance, the way we set out to render "Flight of the Bumblebee" and "Malegueña". But my piano and I put a charm on my father's steel cabinets and exacto blades, my mother's baskets, made of stained and dyed grasses and reed from the Indian reservation on Walpole Island. In the course of my piano lessons I had to come to terms with the basement, with its collection of previous endeavors.

My father's hobbies were never swept up when he began the next, so ping pong table took over shuffle board set, electric train mounted work bench, desk and a telephone buried wash tubs, and all my dolls and play dishes lay on the bottom layer. We had survived World War II by these means: playing games and building paper airplanes, purchasing Rita Hayworth and Lana Turner posters, (my father bought them and also white tap shoes and records of Benny Goodman and Spike Jones; we had boxes of coupon booklets and stacks of magazines, my mother was an inveterate reader of magazines). We had survived the war.

But Miss Gostelow, knowing none of this and not wanting me to proceed with my musical education in any way unseemly, tried to keep me from my father's Jerome Kern and "chopsticks." She assigned music that was cold and uncharming. She didn't trust me to Chopin or Mozart. Bach was too difficult so she gave me Couperin and Czerny scales and exercises, a little bit of the romantic composers, and the Russians in dreadfully watered-down versions with bouncing left hand drudgery and simple work for the right hand. But I was one of those who wanted to be transformed. Dangerous to myself, I already had aspirations, how had Mozart's sister done it? Where was the perfect gratuitousness which was music? For if in myself I possessed a desert country, how was I to bring about its heyday?

We always began the piano lessons in the same way, I sitting down at the bench in front of the keys and placing one of the yellow-covered books on the music rack. Often, I had not practiced. I found it hard to discipline myself to a daily regimen although, in the beginning, I mastered the music because I saw myself going through a procedure which told me I was a pianist. There were many months, even years, when I practiced consistently a little at a time each day as she'd advised me, but toward the last, when I was in my last year of high school, I began more and more to take from her person, her devotion to an art or way of life.

My progress would therefore be spotty and, in order to distract her, I would notice that somebody had forgotten to put water in the dish on the radiator or, most often, I might encourage her to talk about her past.

She had gone to school in Chicago, this was at Northwestern, probably fifty years ago, and one winter, before exams, she went shopping with a college friend and absentmindedly took hold of her friend's arm. What had ensued, which bothered Miss Gostelow so much, was that her friend pulled her arm away and said, "Don't do that."

When she told me this I remember exactly what I thought. I remember thinking about two women, arm in arm, looking in store windows one winter twilight. They were good friends. I lost myself in the happiness of that moment and I was concerned that Miss Gostelow's feelings had been hurt. But to never touch her friend again!

There I was down in the basement, playing the piano even though my nose was cold and there was dust all over everything while my parents ignored me and the music I was making. I felt so much sympathy for Miss Gostelow I immediately made a vow never to pull my arm away. This question of intimacy. It was a hard one.

One day we—I must have been taking lessons for years now—were just beginning in this vein, Miss Gostelow going coolly to the little card table and taking my dollar and a half as always and reaching for her brown Parker to write out the receipt—she had beautiful penmanship—when the door chimes rang. The windows were covered by white Venetian blinds, usually half closed. There were two portraits facing the piano, one of her father, a dentist, and the other of the composer Godowski. These men had witnessed a few years back my complete inability to distinguish a waltz from four-four time. This had been one of several intellectual lapses which burned me to a crisp. It had been so embarrassing I wondered whether it precluded music lessons entirely.

But the door chimes rang. I remember Miss Gostelow put down the pen and uncrossed her feet–she was wearing black suede heels–and stood up to go, her blouse front a mass of laces that stirred like living things and I smelled her odor like the hungry child I was, odor of aged newsprint mixed with perfume. With great curiosity and excitement Miss Gostelow wondered aloud who could be ringing the chimes, on the quarter hour.

My father was driven crazy by having to wait outside on the front curb for me to exit her house always a little late but supposedly at quarter to the hour. I heard Miss Gostelow talking to someone in the ante-room by the front door but this was not my father. She was talking in a hoarse voice and I realized somebody was pushing inside her living room who didn't belong.

"Here, no. You shouldn't," Miss Gostelow said.

"Yes, I am," said one boy.

"That was just what I was getting at," the other one answered with a snarl.

They were one high school and one grade school boy. Both of them were trying to collect money but the older one was the most rude.

"I'm sorry," said the smaller one gazing at Miss Gostelow and holding some pamphlets. He had little skinny fingers, wrinkled like a crab's.

"What's the matter with you?" the loutish one in a greasy jacket said and he slammed the little boy so hard he made an awful noise.

"Please leave," said Miss Gostelow. "I don't want to buy anything." She continued to stand there while her head wobbled back and forth like a marionette while they exited. Then she bent over the rug trying to pick up clumps of mud. It was wintertime and they had been wet, cold, and steamy.

When she came back, her feet padded on the carpet and her head still jiggled slightly from side to side.

"Let's hear your music." I felt her behind my back, her abdomen and a suede belt, her blouse and black skirt all announced themselves to me, although my back was turned. She shook out a lace hanky.

I bent over the piano and began to play. The Chickering had a firmer action than my wild piano of loose ancestry and the keys were apt to go slippery on me. Nevertheless I did the best I could playing with exactness but feeling, as she advised me, while I felt my face and hands growing hot.

When I finished she was sitting down and her face was dark with an odd angry expression.

I turned a page. The old pattern of late winter afternoons began, the carpet blending into the whispering traffic on Michigan Avenue which was the cars of the four o'clock shift automobile factory workers.

Miss Gostelow had been badly disturbed. Many things disturbed her nowadays. She was apt to think she needed protection where no threat occurred. She talked about the way meat was butchered and lobsters were boiled alive. She believed fluoride was bad for you if it were put in the public drinking water. She loved Eisenhower. "He is a great man," she would say, "and I am afraid the office of President has exhausted him." She was exceedingly concerned about Catholics.

I could scarcely understand this, except that it was eccentric. My mother thought Miss Gostelow exceedingly eccentric.

Miss Gostelow had been holding herself so rigidly that now, when she thought to relax, her lap convulsed and the skirt moved. But just as suddenly, she began to want to talk and to be happy.

"Is your boyfriend coming to get you?"

"Oh," I said, "wait, no. I think not today, but I've brought my school yearbook."

It was a thin butter-colored book with a spaceship. I was embarrassed of it, now that I saw it in Miss Gostelow's hands. She looked through the pages with interest, however, until at the end she came to the handwritten note.

It was one of those high school things written by a boy.

"Your friend?" she said.

"No," I answered but it was and I quickly turned over the page.

Miss Gostelow shuffled through the book again before handing it back.

I knew that she knew I was hiding the note from her eyes. I remembered the many years ago when my father first took me as a child to her house, and how she had received him with a fluttered girlish politeness. It was that sort of dishonesty. Being not quite real. But what could Miss Gostelow know of my necking in the car with Kilroy or my feelings when I touched him?

When the little square notes used to skip off the table and land on the carpet Miss Gostelow made a big childish shriek. She loved to laugh. I would always pick up the notes that fell in those days because my fingers were so young. And it always seemed even back then that it had been hard for Miss Gostelow to put her thumb and finger together because, as she said, of the accident.

We didn't know what the accident had been. She spoke of it so solemnly none of her students dared ask. I thought maybe she had caught her hand in a lawn mower. Miss Gostelow did yard work.

The landscape over the card table was one where you could skip over fallen leaves down a sun splotched sidewalk while the receipts were being written. In all these years she must have written thousands of them. Except I never took piano lessons in the summer. This had always been a struggle between us because Miss Gostelow believed musical ability was lost by not playing for three months. Her dining room had been the setting for some subtle conflicts, most of them enacted in elaborate tones between a seventy year old woman standing dominant at the portrait of Godowski and a fifteen year old girl.

Since the accident Miss Gostelow did not play anymore. I never heard her play one of my pieces. She had either to tell me how to play it or I had to attempt it myself not knowing exactly how it should sound. The hand that had been hurt was stiff, I could see that. Once in a while Miss Gostelow took it and lifted it above the keys and let it sink feelingly into the phrases. I thought it sounded good, good enough for her to continue, but she wouldn't. She would shake her head and cease to play. Both her hands were short and full-fleshed, not the thin hands of an old woman. I felt that she had hurt her hand sometime in the years when she was already old but before I began taking lessons. I could not imagine a young Miss Gostelow with this hurt hand. She was too free. She had never acquired the habit of being disabled.

When she signed the receipts she did not move her fingers at all. She moved the hand all together from the elbow and let her arm drop to the table the way she said you should if you were trying to get volume out of the base notes without getting harshness.

Sometimes my eyes needed a rest from looking at Miss Gostelow too long. Sometimes they crossed. I made my eyes go back and forth across Miss Gostelow's face from right eye to left so I wouldn't go cross-eyed. Sometimes I put my eyes on the space right above Miss Gostelow's nose.

Implausible things threatened her, a burglar who might break in through a window or a phone call when the caller hung up. She would tell me these things and I began to recognize a certain fear that was unfounded. And of course the friend who took her arm or was it that she had taken the friend's arm? Anyway the friend had said, "Don't do that," and Miss Gostelow had been deeply hurt. She said she understood or at least she never touched that friend again. "Some people don't like to be touched," she explained to me.

Miss Gostelow would not kill any living thing except moths. She would catch a fly in a bottle and let it go outdoors and the same with any kind of insect. On the other hand, if she saw a moth she would kill it between her hands because a moth can ruin a piano.

"A moth is death to a piano, not to mention the carpets."

When a moth appeared in the room, or, at least, Miss Gostelow said there was one, we would kneel and hunt under the table and around the piano legs. I would hunt for it as long as she wanted me to and then, getting up, check that the pan of water on the radiator was not dry. That was her other fear: that the felts in the piano would dry out.

But the day came when I began to separate myself from her. I couldn't even help it because I was in high school and very busy. Somehow I couldn't tell Miss Gostelow that I wouldn't be taking piano anymore. In the next room the little blond boy in a sailor suit was climbing a fence. He wouldn't help me. He wore a pancake hat and was not quite smiling. Or was he? There were frills at his cuffs and one leg had already hopped over because, Miss Gostelow said, that had been the only way they could get him to hold still.

On top of all else, that summer not only did she want me to take lessons through the summer but she wanted me to increase my lessons to twice a week. So I took the lessons. There were two other girls she wanted me to practice with as a trio. Miss Gostelow thought I couldn't because of money so she offered to give the extra lesson free and make it on an afternoon when there were no other lessons following so that I could stay longer. I was feeling roped-in.

The other girls were Marsha and Mary. Marsha was dark and gentle, somewhat vague. Mary was a Catholic and Miss Gostelow believed that Catholics confessed everything to the Priest and thus nothing was safe with them. Otherwise, Mary was her favorite even though Mary was mischievous enough to have said, "Why don't you play for us today, Miss Gostelow?" and looked sidewise at us as she said it.

After the other girls left I knew I must tell her that after these next few weeks I was going to stop taking piano lessons. "I don't think I should be taking lessons this fall," I said rather abruptly but not knowing how else to begin. Miss Gostelow looked at me. "I am so busy, I have a schedule of things at school." I saw she wasn't following. "I've got clubs and a boyfriend."

Horrid look. We stared at one another. I felt the way you do when a puzzle starts to fall apart if it is lifted. I began to cry and had to go to find my jacket in the vestibule. I stayed in there a minute. I couldn't find a handkerchief so I wiped my nose on my hem. Then I made myself go back, passing on the way the set of *Young Musicians*. She had never let me play Chopin.

"Is there something wrong...your mother?" Miss Gostelow believed my mother was to blame for everything. "Some reason you must stop taking lessons?"

"No," I said, "it is just what I said. That I am busy and ... sorry." I repeated again the reason, saying it so softly and humbly I hoped Miss Gostelow would see that I was making an offering to her the way wild animals do to each other. I was offering the little, delicate meat of my desire to do what I wanted and counting on Miss Gostelow to say 'yes,' to let me go. And after serving myself up in this way, I had expected, or perhaps not, that it would be easier. Anyway, Miss Gostelow felt tricked. Anger came over her face.

"Well, then," she said, "do so." And she got up and walked to the vestibule and shoved open the door.

"Here are your books. Well, goodbye"

And that was it.

I found myself out on the porch with the sign: Anne Gostelow, Teacher of Piano. I didn't suspect her anger would endure, she was my teacher, had taught me more about life and music than anyone else.

After a few weeks a letter came. My mother showed it to me. I was surprised because it was as if Miss Gostelow were still thinking over the conflict, had not resolved it–she could remember many more of the details than I could–and so I caught the actual thought process. She was still angry and hurt. I felt nine hundred miles away, like an orphan. She wrote again and then once again. It was at Christmas. She sent us an elaborate card of a piano keyboard and beautiful sprigs of holly and just the name, printed.

She left no survivors. They bulldozed her house. That's Lansing for you. That is modern day itself, isn't it? And, yes, it is absolutely true that I've become an artist. It's as if I've practiced all my life wanting to take someone's arm but not doing it.

The Dreams of My Father

My father, in the 1940s, was an inventor. He invented the safe box. It was supposed to be secure against fires and floods. We had not heard of, or considered, worse catastrophes back then. The safe box was, in reality, a simple cement block with a steel door you could lock. He always intended to invent the circular hot dog bun and gloves that drew on and then 'firmed up', as well as pencils with a hollow end. (He had one with a cement block–the safe box–in it, that shifted back and forth inside the pencil like a birdie with an air bubble.) An inventor may define his terrain.

His inventiveness must have been inherited. My grandfather made automobile trash receptacles on the principle of saddles that had sand bags in them, and he got a patent. Neither he nor my father was ever concerned about how things ought to be done. My father put things together 'cold'. He did not care how the directions read.

He invented a fishing rod with a bell that would call him from whatever he was doing. He designed and made a carrying seat for me that attached to the front fender of his bicycle. I remember a safety bar that swung across my stomach and locked. That was during World War II when we didn't have a car.

To the last of his life, he was delighted with things like water monkeys, secret passageways, whistles and harmonicas and wheels in general. He liked stringed instruments you could redesign by removing the bridge and carving the inside over again. He was fascinated with perspective because it was that perfect combination of the miracle: objects drawing closer together the further you got from them.

If you bought him slippers, he would take out scissors and design them over again. He did the same with belts. He made me a playhouse out of a refrigerator box, a scooter out of roller skates, a train out of a wagon and some tubes. I thought he was going about it wrong. I would rather have had a new scooter. But, in retrospect, I see that I share his independence; and his impatience to do something quickly, in his own way, is also mine.

I was born early in the stages of World War II when he was thinking about going to war and before he found that he was 4F. He wanted my mother all to himself. Otherwise why would he buy her the satin peach colored nightgowns and the rabbit skin bathrobe, the white figure skates? And I came along, possessive, intense, and wanting something.

He thought life should be easy. In exchange for that illusion, which allowed him to invent so many things, he remained a child. He didn't like to take the trouble to change. He was the youngest member of the high school band, allowed to join when he was still in seventh grade, but he couldn't read music.

He inflated balloons at the lake and set them afloat so we could practice bows and arrows. He set us up with horse shoes in the back yard and later with an archery field.

He was especially sensitive to small creatures. He was aware of rabbits and moths, birds of all kinds and of course the squirrels which lived in our rather civilized, suburban neighborhood. I remember in particular a time he noticed a squirrel was caught in our neighbor's upstairs attic. Somehow the squirrel had gotten trapped inside and could be seen from our house peering out the dormer window. In order to rid himself of squirrels, our neighbor had installed a trap door that opened out, and when he was certain all the squirrels were gone he had screened up the opening.

But my father had seen one more. After a sleepless night, he decided to talk to the neighbor and convinced him to go up on a ladder and rescue the squirrel. And then he reported to me how the rescue attempt went.

"Mr. Jones went up there on his ladder and sure enough he took the screen and door off so the squirrel could come out but that crazy squirrel instead of jumping to the pine tree and coming down the way the rest of them had done somehow missed the branch and fell headfirst, missing the fir trees that it might have held on to. And it fell flat and just lay there." So my father said.

"But suddenly the squirrel seemed to revive because it stood up. And then it screamed something."

"I'm free, I'm free, I'm free!" is what my father heard.

🙟 🙟 🙟

He hated to see changes of age in himself. By the 1980s this was trembling hands, graying hair, diminished sight, people thinking of him as a grandpa. He was never able to believe he was getting old. Like Great-Grandpa Halsey, catching sight of his own reflection in the drugstore, he didn't recognize himself. He always saw life from the eyes of someone on the verge of adulthood. That was his magic.

"Who *is* that old man?" Great Grandpa Halsy had said. "He looks familiar. I must know him."

One Christmas he told us a dream. We were sitting in the small living room. I remember he sat hunched over and his head lifted every time he took a breath. He was breathing through the clear tubes. His hands dangled between his legs and I saw the gold band of his wedding ring. His fingers were muscular and square like my own.

"I was sleeping," my father began. "And somehow I knew I was dying. So I tried to call to Catherine. She was asleep and I found I couldn't make a sound. I tried and tried, but no sound came out. I couldn't even grunt."

"'Wow', I thought, 'they make it hard for you when you are dying. Can't even talk to anyone.'"

"I had something I wanted to say," he went on, "but I couldn't even so much as move my hands or turn my head. I wanted to shake Catherine and say, 'Hey. Wake up. I have just had a dream that I am dying.'"

"But I could move one finger. Just this one, the index finger on my right hand, at the tip. I remembered the Morse Code I learned in Boy Scouts so I tapped on the headboard. 'Catherine?' maybe I said, or I said, 'Help Help.' And she heard me and woke up. 'I didn't think I could get through to you,' I said."

"'Well, you did,' she answered and laughed."

≥   ≥   ≥

My memories of him unravel. I remember how the clear plastic tubes came from his nostrils, met on his chest and became one, then wound down to the floor where we tried not to step on them. These tubes had to be jerked and coiled like a lasso out of the way. The main tube led down a hall where it hooked up to a huge tank in the bedroom. This breathing tank made soothing sounds like an aquarium. In order to take away an empty tank and replace it with a full one, a delivery truck had to come once a week.

My father was always very nervous about hooking up to a new source. Sometimes after they left, the valves would stick. He might have to make some adjustment and we would find him sitting on the edge of the bed gasping for breath and trying to twist and turn the valves. His arms and fingers would be visibly shaking and his lips and whole face dark red. Then he would give up.

If my mother couldn't do it, we would have to call the personnel and ask them.

"It's jammed," they said when they got there. "This screw somehow got stripped." Or, they might respond with some other kind of matter-of-fact statement, which made my father's desperation all the more evident.

After he died, but before the personnel knew of it, they came to make a delivery and my mother met them at the door, She was trying to let them down gently.

"Bill isn't here. He's died," she said.

They were not expecting her to say this and so they stood on the porch for a moment with the replacement. Finally they left, but in a few days they had to make a return trip for the equipment which included the portable stroller my father had used in the early days. Its original smallish wheels had been put away because he had engineered large, lightweight ones for it. The wheels looked suspiciously like the ones on my scooter.

My mother decided to keep those wheels and let them have the small ones back. Then, after they took out the big tank in the bedroom, she put the valet there and hung an afghan over it.

Victor, my father's only living uncle, was not expecting the news either. He called as usual to inquire about the events of the week and, being over eighty, couldn't understand it when it was explained to him.

"Bill passed away," one of us said.

"What?" Victor evidently replied.

"He passed away. Yesterday. Thursday."

Poor soft-hearted Victor, Victor cried when he had to give away his last cow. He couldn't understand. Not William, not his nephew. Why, William had learned to shoot his first BB gun out at the farm. Victor was sorry for William because he was from city folks.

🙵 🙵 🙵

My father always owned bird feeders. They drew mostly black birds, jays, and house sparrows because our suburb lacked trees. The birds which came were evidence of a brutal predominance of take-over species. (I include squirrels.) But my father never recognized the principle of hegemony and was prone to admire these few as much as any. He would take six or eight pieces of perfectly good bread, tear them up, and give them to the birds in addition to all the seed, suet, and sweetened water, and, of course, this caused a rampage. He had to arrange the feeders near the window so he could watch and supervise if it were necessary.

My father is buried in Evergreen Cemetery. My brother also is buried there, with the babies. And, finally, of course, even my brother Don is buried there. The graves of my grandfather and grandmother are behind a stone I can always find which reads: TRUMP.

And over a slight rise, hangs a medium-sized tree. Its branches hang down just right for a bird feeder. This is where my father is buried.

🙵 🙵 🙵

He grew very weak. My mother took to sleeping sitting up in the next room. There were two recliner chairs. My father would sit in one with everything he needed within arm's reach. He usually sat there in the evening. An old smoke stand with copper lining sat next to him and the brown-glass ash tray rested on top. My father had always had this ashtray and it was probably representative of his downfall. The smoke stand's doors opened one at a time, I remember, and inside there were pipe cleaners and a rack of pipes. Because of the copper, it looked like a miniature mirrored room that smelled like my father.

The collection of objects which he kept around him and which he had either made himself or needed within reach was as follows: a dulcimer and banjo (under the chair), a guitar, a harmonica, a lava lamp, a carved wooden sea captain, a paint-by-number ship at sea, a tile elephant which looks as though he is stepping on the picture frame and breaking it (my father's idea), a battery-operated razor, and a set of pajamas. It was in this room, while sleeping, that my mother also had a dream.

"I dreamed," she said, "that I was a student in a school that had a long hall and cloak rooms. The hall had doors opening on it with windows in them. Someone was going from door to door and peering at me through the windows. I was sure he was going to catch me but I saw double doors at the end of the hall. They were hard to push open but I ran down the hall anyhow. I knew I had made a mistake though because I saw that he could get me from any of the side doors. I wouldn't have time to make it down to the end of the hall. He would be able to push a door and get me. He was just doing that when I screamed."

"At first, I couldn't make much noise, but then I made a kind of gargle in my throat and then I really screamed. I must have screamed loud because Bill woke up and came in and shook me and told me I was screaming. Now isn't that strange? What could I have been frightened of?"

But my mother is like that. She kept going back and forth between saying "we" and "I" now that he is gone. She kept saying she needed to do something for him as if he were with her. She answered the phone talking "we" so I was not surprised that she relayed her dream as if it was something that had dropped down into her life earlier when she had had nothing special to be frightened of. All this denial business is a familiar characteristic on her side of the family. I had taught myself to beware of it. Otherwise, I would think that my eyes were deceiving me, but still I was accused of being too ... too what? too much trouble I guess. Too mean.

Soon after, my father began to withdraw from everyone but my mother. When my sister came to visit and tried to do things for him he didn't want her to. He was in bed at that time. She said she brought his supper one night on a tray and she brought a glass of water but he said, "Is this water cold enough? Are you sure? You had better get Catherine to come in here and get me another glass."

He did not want her to go away during the day either. One morning my mother was out when someone called. When she came back, my father told her that the phone had rung and rung and, boy was he put out!

"There were seventeen or eighteen calls."

"Well, who was it?" my mother asked.

He said that it was my sister.

"She called that many times?"

"Well ...no," he said. "Just once."

"Who was it all of the other times?" she asked.

He didn't know, but it had rung.

He said, "Catherine, if I need to tell you something, I want you to be here. I think I might have something I want to tell you. Will you hear me from the bedroom? Maybe we should get a little bell that I can ring. Do you think so?"

My mother said, "No, Bill, I do not think so."

❧   ❧   ❧

In the mornings, he would sit at the kitchen table and make things until lunch which took an hour, and then he would go slowly into the bedroom for a nap, dragging his air hose behind him. He didn't like to get it caught on something. If you stood on it and he moved, it would jerk his nose.

He built things out of balsa wood and craft sets. He built twirling Christmas trees out of tongue depressors and painted them jade and hung them outside near the bird feeders. He had his wind machines; one was of a boy sawing wood. He had a whole file cabinet of supplies–duck decoys and wood chains and sharp knives and cans of putty and paint.

He watched a TV show on how to paint with oils. He was fascinated by winter landscapes with the tips of black fence posts in the fields. He liked to see them disappear according to the laws of perspective.

"They make it look so easy," he would say.

❧   ❧   ❧

After my brother Doug drowned, when I was ten years old, my father ripped out the pages of the Bible from the Gospel of Matthew.

These were the passages which said if you asked for anything, you would get it.

Although the bottom fell out of his belief, he didn't actually lose his faith because the last winter I visited, he asked me questions about what I thought of prayer. He wanted to know if my brother was in heaven did I think? Then he told me he did not imagine him as grown-up, as he must be by now, but rather that he thought of him as being about two, which was how old he was the day he died, or, maybe a few years older, he conceded. Then he asked me whether I thought people should pray for someone to re-marry if they have gotten divorced.

"Should I pray for that?" he asked. "And, maybe Dougie sees, maybe he sees people who have died, do you think so? But, do you think I should pray?"

At Christmas he taught me again how to memorize so that I could remember up to forty names. It could be more he, told me, if I would just think of a picture to go with it. His fingers were fluttery, I noticed, when he drew the pictures that went with the names. The wedding band was loose. A small halo. It shone with a golden and unscratched purity.

My mother told him goodbye alone at the funeral home after everyone else had left. I saw her, but I ducked out. I could see his hands were crossed and the wedding band was on his finger. I only looked briefly. I remembered impatient trembling hands holding down the keys on the saxophone or playing the piano or drawing pictures for me.

He had wanted at the end for it to be simply the two of them.

"Catherine, do I need a little bell?"

"No, Bill," she had said. "I don't think you do. Honestly."

"I know that old man but I can't think of his name," old Great-Grandpa Halsey had said referring to himself in the mirror. "My, he has aged!" My father was childlike and funny like that about himself.

At the funeral we asked for Carols because it was Christmas. I asked for the Song of Solomon from the Bible too, for the marriage verses, but the minister had something else. Still, it was okay because I could remember my father as he was. When he played

"Silent Night" his cheeks puffed out, his eyes bugged, and his arms and hands poured into the instrument as if trying to approximate the perfection he heard in his head.

> ❧   ❧   ❧

My best friend, Sarah Jane, and I were movie crazy. The Gladmere Theater in town played *Show Boat* and the Lansing Theater showed *Annie Get Your Gun,* and we would see them three and four times. Then we put on high heels and old dresses and acted them out. We especially liked movies about airline crashes in the jungles where we married the pilot and the co-pilot in a double-ring ceremony.

The day we acted *The Greatest Show on Earth* was one of those days. We had gotten bored and decided to go into the bathroom to practice our tight rope walking by balancing on the edge of the bathtub. We were too grown-up that day to be able to find anything to do. I remember that my mother asked if we wanted to color and we said No! Anyhow, we hung onto the towel bars and by mistake we jerked too hard and pulled one of them out of the plaster. The hole in the wall horrified my mother and she put us together, two grown girls, in one big overstuffed chair to wait for my father. We sat there, twelve years old, and it was not lost on us how we had felt so grown up and how funny it was, that we were sitting there, but we were also terribly worried about the damage, what my father might do or say.

My mother explained it to him. She was still mad. My father must have found it a little hard to connect with. At least, he couldn't work up any anger and finally, seeing that my mother wanted him to do something, he said, "Just don't do that again."

He liked movies too, he was a child too. He had played dance bands at a club called Orion Lake and had worn white tap shoes. We even had a picture of him, with his group, all dressed like Benny Goodman in white pants.

So the week the Capitol building partially burned I thought, naturally, of the movie *Quo Vadis.* I asked my father since my mother was out that night if it meant the end of the world. He said, no that he thought the fire department would have it out by midnight, perhaps sooner, and that I should go to bed. I was rather surprised that he didn't get my gist about *Quo Vadis* but he was tired. Except for the search light on the Capitol building and the hook and ladder truck and the lights at the Civic Center where my mother wa singing with the Mother Singers, everything in town was dark.

ɜ⋆   ɜ⋆   ɜ⋆

The first time he ever tried to discipline me didn't work out. I wanted a drink of water and I asked for it over and over. It was my way of being playful. I remember thinking, "Come here to me, you parents, I want to see you in the dark."

But they didn't want to see me and finally my father was selected to come. He spanked me and when I didn't stop crying he got mad and left the room. Well, that was all a misunderstanding, wasn't it? I had wanted to see their faces, that was all. I was usually a very somber child and when the playful moods came, they were rare and took me to a peak.

I have another memory. My father is sleeping with his arm over me. I am about four. He has left it there by mistake and I am supposed to be taking a nap but I am not. I have to pretend to be asleep but I don't know why. I have to be completely still and breathe as if I am sleeping. I am susposed to be a very good little girl. So I even let my chest rise and fall. Then I want to swallow. I must.

I know that people do not swallow when they are sleeping but I have to. I do it. There. Immediately, I have to swallow again.

A cat appeared at the window on the other side of the screen. I remember this because it was an all-knowing cat that knew all about me and was watching. Just watching. My father's arm is like lead. If I had been really sleeping, I could have shrugged his arm off and pulled away or rolled over. But, instead, I am pretending, so I am trapped. Only the cat is watching.

ɜ⋆   ɜ⋆   ɜ⋆

My father began to drink. I was not supposed to tell my Grandma. Grandma Messenger would not have cared but I could not tell the other side of the family. It felt like he had gone from us, even further than he already was. And then he began to offer drinks to my mother and she took them.

I could never say the word "alcoholic". I never could say comfortably the word "drown". And somehow even if I could say that my father was an alcoholic, I could never admit that my mother was. Nevertheless, if the emphysema hadn't killed him the alcohol would have.

        ಎ   ಎ   ಎ

The streets in Lansing were named after trees and Indians. My father had worked for the Fisher Body Plant and attended the land grant college. He had dated girls on Sycamore Street and played in the parades on Ottawa and Washtenaw and Shiawassee, when he was a young man.

The main corners were a situation of banks and dentist's offices and a Mr. Peanut, wobbling and coming along toward you if you made the mistake of going on that side of the street. On the Capitol building lawn there was a streaked bronze monument of the first Michigan Sharpshooters.

So when, in 1985, the hearse moved, in not exactly princely fashion, through deep snow past the monument, the play ground where I thought people got polio, and the main corners, my sister and mother and I recognized these places from years back, but kept our eyes on the gladiolus pressed in the back window of the hearse where my father was.

        ಎ   ಎ   ಎ

My mother had bought him, as a last birthday present, a garage door opener and she called a local carpenter to come and install it but our garage had been made by my father and it had an unusual, non-conforming ceiling and so the door opener was difficult to install.

After awhile my father looked in on the job, this was in the days just before he stopped walking but had to lean on something, and he found the carpenter gone and his son, a boy in his late teens, sitting on the floor surrounded by his tools and crying.

This upset my father so much that he almost ran to tell my mother.

"Guess what?" he would have said, gasping for breath. "I went to check on the carpenter and…"

The two of them sat and thought about it, in the room with the recliner chairs, my mother wanting none of it, my father panting and finally going back out to him.

"There," he told the young carpenter, "don't worry. We will figure how to install it. I will think about it and when I have, I will call you and you can come out and try again."

>= >= >=

The day he died was the day he was going for tests at the hospital. He thought he could find out if something could be done to make him more comfortable. He was expecting us at Christmas again and maybe he was thinking of that. They decided to go–it was hard getting him into the car. He never went anywhere by then–even the barber came to the house–but he died while the doctor was inserting the tube into his lung (it had hurt always, but it was a procedure he knew). My mother reports that suddenly it happened just like that. He said, "Oh!" and that was all.

It was a surprise I suspect that death came or otherwise he would have had something more to tell her: "Catherine? I had that dream. Do you remember? We were in the bed."

Tirade

I am not one of those people who quickly understands, my mother said. I figure it out later. I am like my own mother-in-law who called herself a slow thinker. One time she was robbed of one hundred fifty dollars right out of her purse. The purse was behind her bed. She had left her apartment in a retirement home and gone downstairs to eat. The money had been in the purse a long time. Set aside. Fifty dollars of it was from my father-in-law and he had been dead eleven years. I thought that served her right. But she thought differently. Anyhow, that is not why she called herself a slow thinker and not why she didn't recognize a mistake. That has to do with the fact that some months later the burglar was caught. He turned out to have been a twenty-three year old man with debts. I am quoting her. (I thought he must have been a drug addict.) Anyhow, with debts to pay, she understood that.

She couldn't understand his way of accumulating so many debts and not paying them but she is eighty-eight and can't remember a time when she wasn't comfortable. She didn't even suffer during the depression. While my mother was baking fudge to sell and giving it to my father to take to work, she still had a cleaning lady. While I and my sisters were sharing two white blouses and a dark skirt between us and washing them out every night so we could go to work or college–but that is not what I am driving at.

I didn't get to stay in my high school in order to graduate because we had to move in the last half of my senior year. I never had my teeth straightened. I was not able to finish the last term of college because the Depression hit–the term where I would have done an internship as a med tech in a hospital. I got married in a little bitty ceremony in a brown dress and a dark brown hat, gosh it was depressing, and my mother-in-law cried all the way through it. I've never been to such a sad wedding!

What I am driving at is that my mother-in-law received a telephone call from someone connected to the burglary case and his reason for calling was to ask her how she wanted the burglar punished.

Now, she was not expecting to be consulted and even if she had been, she was not prepared for an answer. So she told the caller not to do anything to the man. She said, "Do nothing," and hung up and then she called me on the phone and said, "I thought immediately I should have said, 'He ought to pay me back the one hundred-fifty dollars.'"

I thought that was exactly the right thing to say too. But we both thought of it too late. 'Maybe this is a new way of justice, my mother-in-law went on,'to ask the victim what the punishment should be. Anyway I wasn't prepared for it.'

Recently I went out in a boat, my mother went on. It was only a matter of time before I saw ripples and thought, I ought to have a fishing pole. Well there was one in the boat, dusty, not working well, but I fished and I caught one bluegill. Or, at least, that is what we call them in Michigan. I had a potato chip plastic pail and I filled it with water and put the fish in. I took it home. I didn't catch any other. So it was still alive and Bill took it and drove a spike in it and killed it and cut off the tail and head and cleaned out the insides and we put it in the freezer all small and alone to wait for others. But we never did catch any more. One day I put it together with some canned fish chowder and made a soup.

It cooked away and I was able to remove the back bone and all the little bones. When it came dinner time I had other left-overs to serve and I ate those. The fish soup I could have eaten but instead I gave it to my husband.

It was bluegill soup. He said so and he was right.

"I notice you didn't eat any bluegill soup," he said to me.

"That wasn't bluegill soup," I said, "that was fish stew. That was just a fish soup."

But I knew it was bluegill and I had never in all my life ever heard of a meal called that. The one little bluegill. It reminded me of 'making do', the one little useless bluegill and of the Depression–and now that's over I'm not going back!

Aunt Mildred's Bike

Rain makes me want to put on a bathing suit and run in the rain. I want to go immediately outside and run among the trees. Other people say oh it is so damp it is so cold and I myself say yes isn't it lovely? I stand and watch water pour down the drain and the funnels. I watch lightning stab and sear the sky.

Why didn't Jesus say the mass in rain I wonder. Gorse rain, jungle rain, fidgeting rain, scuttling rain, rain before you whose beauty shall-be-a-sheet-before-me while we are like goats in it. The rain flying nails and timber, rain rocking itself, going under a bridge skewered angered sullen, rain biting against the rain stuff in another language. Rain on a lake–gray rain to gray warm–while I bound for home and dry clothes and a nap.

Am I sad because of losing the day on the lake drowning me with itself or of the survival of me and the loss of the day, all the love like a bike in reserve on the back porch?

❧ ❧ ❧

In every child, a tiger. In every child a tiger walks. Let the child who has not known a tiger, speak. A tiger walks toward home, padding in and out and every child whether or not she has seen one owes her life to there being such.

❧ ❧ ❧

My father's mother's kitchen window had crisscrossed wires and a decal of the Little Dutch Girl. My grandma took me all over the house, talking about what went there and what went here. She showed me the contents of the linen closets, the kitchen cupboards, the game closet, and, my favorite, a napkin drawer where the jade rabbit lived. Jade rabbit with white eyes.

I want that grandmother to tuck me into bed, I want her to wake me with frying bacon and ask me to dry the dishes boiling hot. I want to see my fingers turn red from rinse water and I want her to tell me my suit is on the line, that I can take the canoe. I want to see her standing on the dock telling me I have had too much sun that I may drown so soon after lunch. Then I will say to her rebel-like, "If I don't die of this, of what?"

During the time my mother was pregnant with me, my father made paper airplanes. I climbed the stairs to the attic to see them eye-level, dozens of the gauzy things floating from strings attached to the rafters. There they were, abandoned in the full bloom of completion, while I was free to grow. Why had he left them there?

My father taught me to sing "Silent Night". I felt very important singing this but I had to swallow in the middle of the word "virgin" creating a diphthong. So the beauty of the song as I sang it made my parents laugh.

I climbed a fruit tree on a day growing dark and cold and I prodded a sap button that was orangy and full of fluid, forcing it to give up somewhere.

My parents invited a girl named Isabelle to our home but I refused to speak to her. I remember we sat on the floor of my room for an hour without talking. She must have been quiet like me. I wanted to speak to her. I remember the green patterned linoleum as, all that time I considered, and discarded, 'openers'. Finally it was time for her to go home without our having made friends.

I thought I might be a writer. It was an occupation which was not carried out with friends, which insisted on going solo. Furthermore, it was unnecessary, and yet, to me, flowed like an avenue of joy.

The books in my grandfather's garage smelled of the lake and of something having been saturated and yet were wonderful smelling even as they were turning yellow and crisp like flakes. Some spoke to a more mature person inside me, words said straight into my heart sternly and adult-wise into my center. "We know what we are doing here. We know what we are up to, don't we?" the books said.

I can even think of it now while I remember something I see in my mind–a bicycle on the back porch of our house. It was Aunt Mildred's bike, my mother's sister. Aunt Mildred had lost her husband on Okinawa and lived with us when my mother had a miscarriage.

But why did we have her bicycle? It sat on our porch with its tires collapsed. There was a bike stand for the back wheel. The tires did not look collapsed unless you touched them or you had an analytical mind and saw that the front one was flat so the back one must also be old and worn.

There were cobwebs on the bike and dust, so that its true color was vague. There was a bell the color and sound of bronzed bees, rough and rumbling, and I could feel it when it was forced forward and back. It still rang, ling ling! And I could be lifted to the high seat to ring that bell. But for many years I could not reach the pedals.

I might have driven the back wheel, off the ground as it was, if only I could have reached the pedals but that would have meant sacrificing sitting on the seat as I assumed I was supposed to do. But by standing on the pedals I could drive the back wheel, thus achieving half of what it is like to ride a bicycle.

That is, if the balancing part were left alone. I could not balance. I knew that. The bike was too heavy and too old ever for me to try to pedal unaided in the airy, light, weight of day. I preferred, actually, its 'dry-docked' condition. It was a totally anchored bike, reminding me of the ludicrous desire we have to fly. That this machine could be fleet. That wings could be painted on its heavy steel.

There was a headlight that was buggy and like an eyeball, webby and wise with use, on our porch. This light had the diseased intellect of such battery powered lights, gone to pot. Summer and autumn and winter descended on it. No difference, no matter. Aunt Mildred's bike. Would it come to be mine? With all of its weight and rust? Its chain guard, its crotch-grinding seats, its duality such that I could never sit on it correctly and pedal at the same time?

"The spokes are broken." That is what my mother always said out of all the things she might have. What matter, I wondered, that a few of its spokes were broken? That the bike could be made to go at all seemed dependent on more important matters.

Like a chained dog beside a maple tree it remained, never mounting, never climbing, never moving except its handlebars slowly side to side, its back wheel but never its front, long after Aunt Mildred had moved away and, with new life, married again.

The First Boy

After my father left Fisher Body he went to work for a cement block plant. He was in accounts. Right after the war, houses were cheap and loans were easy, so we bought a house in one of the new subdivisions, with no sidewalks or drainage systems. One of the horrors was the possibility of falling where floodwater drained and I remember my mother starting out one evening after supper for a PTA meeting and coming back wet having fallen in over her hips in an uncompleted drain.

The first day of school we had a flood and the water came in under the door of the classroom. It was dark behind the teacher's desk almost like blood. We were excused.

The houses were each a little different. Otherwise, I don't know how I would have come home to the right one. Ours had the picture window and the door in the middle, four rooms, one bath and a full basement. The basement was the thing–all the neighbors were wild to make rec rooms out of them, except us. In our basement we had laundry tubs and the old gas cook stove and picnic baskets, and my upright piano. My father had his tools, his ping pong table, his shuffle-board court and his train set. The upright got so damp the keys went down and stayed.

The boy next door was named Lanny. **His** house had a fireplace and a brick front and the chimney going up the face of the house. Otherwise, the same four rooms and basement. These houses had full attics. They were made into second and third bedrooms. All that separated Lanny's bedroom from mine was a driveway and a thin strip of grass. My girl friend, Sarah Jane, and I used to dress-up in the bedroom in her Aunt Bobbie's clothing because Aunt Bobbie was a shoe size 4. We had a box that contained little pique summer suits, and old negligee's with fluff that were extremely uncomfortable and tangled up in our legs if we slept in them, and little high heeled shoes which Aunt Bobbie had so much trouble finding and that she would pay a lot of money for.

We used to put on make-up and act out parts in movies in my bedroom not realizing that Lanny, probably without even intending to, could watch.

I don't remember meeting Lanny for the first time at all and his life so close next to mine fades in and out for long periods. Sometimes complete years have gone by when I was not for one minute aware of him. Then something would happen and there he was causing me trouble.

When we first moved in to this new house at three-one-two-three Sablain Parkway Drive, I was doing a lot of roller skating. I had terrible bloody knees that summer. Lanny moved in after us but I didn't see him because he had mumps and couldn't come outside. He didn't join me in the sport of roller skating at all. Perhaps he looked too funny long after the mumps subsided. Perhaps Lanny didn't care what he looked like. I've been fortunate enough not to have mumps.

Although my mother didn't think so, Lanny was very attractive. He had a way of smiling and squinting with his bulbous nose and prominent cheekbones and full mouth and small blue eyes. He was short and stocky and I knew he would look exactly like his father someday, who had deep red squint lines and a mechanic's tan. His father was never anything but kind to me as Lanny was. I think I liked them because they were so approachable. They always smiled as I came near and what they had to say was pleasant and easy. "You be good. Take care of yourself now," and so on they would say, implying somehow that I was up to something with that easy familiarity of extroverts.

If I had not been so interested in Lanny, I am sure I would have found him approachable but, as it was, sometimes I couldn't make myself get up the courage to speak to him. So I've only been in Lanny's house a couple of times in all these years.

I'm also very nearsighted. My mother gave me practice doing things in the world to counter my nearsightedness. For example, she instructed me to walk the mile downhill to take the bus to choir practice. She told me what the sign on the bus would say: Soomes Road. I thought the reason I couldn't see it was my own failure. It had not occurred to me that the sign was there in the window and others could read it but that I couldn't see that far. I toyed with the idea that there was some ambiguity involved. Perhaps the sign would say half Soomes Road and half something else the way I saw the street lights half red and half green. Or maybe the driver had forgotten to turn the sign. Then it would display the locale from which he had just come or perhaps that was what it should say, the locale from which it just came; or did it direct the locale in which it was heading? Just what did the sign mean?

But once on this bus I had no problem because it went straight to the main corners of downtown which was a canyon-like place with banks and drugstores and one telegraph office. At that time I didn't have the faintest idea what a telegraph office was. No one in my family had ever received, sent or talked about telegraphs. I expected none ever would receive one in the life allotted the same way none of us had ever flown. Once my grandfather, who was an efficiency expert, went up in a plane and we stood out on the front lawn and waved. The target at which we waved was about the size of a speck on the window.

The state capital was located in our town and that was the reason for the communication services. The bank building was of blue stone, and there were pigeons of a lighter color and a retarded boy who sold *Lansing State Journals* and kept them in an old leather pouch. He and I met more or less at the main corners every Wednesday, he going into the drugstore to get warm and I going into the drugstore, now that I think of it, for the same reason.

I had to go downtown in order to get to choir practice. I had to go across the main corners which were Washington and Michigan and take my bus transfer and hook up with the bus that was going to the church on the north side. This bus was supposed to say either Logan Street or Sparrow Hospital, I can't remember which. It was not possible for my mother to tell me to cross to the north or south/east or west side because I had not mastered such concepts. But she would say, go across to stand by the Michigan National Bank Building, that's the grey building, and wait for a bus that says North Logan. If the bus were parked and I looked right into the front window I could read what the sign said. And I finally learned which side of the main corners she meant—a very cold, windy place on the shaded side. The stores were already failing as they were to do on both sides in the next twenty years. The windows advertised sales and there was yellow cellophane covering the panes. But the real reason I didn't like that side of the street was because the peanut store hired a man to wear a peanut suit, with a huge hard head, to walk up and down the sidewalk, his head bobbing at people.

So I was not happy about moving any distance away from the blue bank building to go over to the Michigan National Bank. But with my transfer I would climb on board—it was a steep climb and hard for all of us—and then I would find a cracked old green seat, slide way in, and put my face near the window.

And as we shook and belched our way north, it would be apparent we were entering an entirely different section of town. This was where I found my church and Sparrow Hospital. Not until now, forty years later, do I really understand that the people who lived here behind or above these storefront buildings and churches were the people from Alabama and Arkansas and Tennessee come up to Michigan to work in the automobile and tool and die factories. In those days, I looked out the dusty windows and I saw people sitting outside and there seemed to be nobody needing to ride this bus but me and the few factory workers who carried their belongings in bags that were suede-soft. I was left to contemplate their workaday fingers and hands—there I was. We didn't have a car and I had to get to choir practice.

I was not sure. But I have thought that these people as they perched on the side seats provided at the front and stared straight out at those on the opposite side must have been people involved in love. And all the hard work didn't quite take it out of them. I thought I should rub my hands together so to speak and get to work on love in my own life. The rattle of the bus, the nausea of the exhaust, the dirt that collected wherever wind and feet allowed caused me to realize I hadn't even touched life.

I remember a man on the bus who was capable of making lightning-quick decisions. He moved over here. Over there. He or some other would savor a good-looking woman. (She would never look back, sitting there, lips the color of lavender, hair in smooth rolls that came behind her ears coquettishly, and large good-looking plastic bracelets on her arms.) She wore a sundress and heels and no nylons and every twitch of her mouth and turn of her head said, "Look at me."

They'd try to flirt with her, whisper something in her ear but she disdained them. Finally, getting up, all eyes upon her, she walked to the front; it was amazing the way she swayed hanging on to the silver chrome pillars and then coming to a stop beside the driver with his box of transfers and money balanced on a pole. She'd wait, resting on one hip, and then descend the steps saying something to the driver.

By comparison, I never knew when it was my stop and I was flung forward and back as I tried to make it to the front of the bus before the driver gave up on me. Yeah, I used to make it to choir practice and not that I sang once I got there. But this was a part of my life lacking Lanny completely. I just mention it.

      ఊ   ఊ   ఊ

I was always crazy about Lanny. He had a neat football jacket and a way of spitting. I didn't even realize he WAS spitting. I just thought whatever it was, was great. He smoked camels and he ran funny, all floppy, and he sat around slouching but yet to grownups he was so polite! He had funny sort of knobby fingers and said, "Girls tell me I have nice hands."

I was getting mosquito bites by then, little nipples, and pubic hair and it bothered me. Sarah Jane and I had evening clothes to wear because we were going to be actresses. On weekends we'd get together, see a movie and then come back and put on the clothes and act the parts in my bedroom. It was as simple as that. We would take off our clothes and throw them in the air and when they came down we would kick them straight up again. We just had a great old time. She used to come over somewhere before the one o'clock matinee on Saturdays and stay overnight. Or I would go to her house. She was richer than I but it didn't matter. Once we went up to her room it was the same old thing, a basket of clothes and the mirror and acting out movies. One time she said, "Let's practice kissing" and she did it. She was taller than me and she took me firmly by the shoulders and she put her lips on mine. It was then I thought, "Well." I could feel her firm lips, dens of slipperiness with spit between them at the cracks, toward the corners. One of us was the woman, and the other the man and we took all sorts of movie roles. We found magic everywhere, in old jewelry, makeup, till there was not one inch more of play and fantasy that needed expression and then we would say goodbye tearfully.

Sarah Jane had real genius and was so smart she could have committed the perfect crime. But in my own way I felt I made a contribution. I made quiet suggestions about whether the stewardesses would marry the co-pilots in the jungle, or later.

When I wasn't playing with Sarah Jane I had to join with the neighborhood kids. They threw jack knifes and kicked the can and made circuses in the garage, planning the three-ring entertainments, even selling tickets. They also played monopoly and card games. Lanny wasn't always a part of this, not because he was shy but because he sometimes had other things he had to do since he was older. I was the one who was shy. My mother used to shove me out the door, even telling me the words I should say to them if they questioned what I was doing there. The words were: Hi, what are you doing? Can I play too?

On one of these occasions I remember Lanny and a few kids were sitting in a circle around a flagpole. They were throwing knives and Lanny looked up at me when I appeared but he was too polite to say anything. One of the few negative things I can ever remember about him was what he said then. He said he didn't like me because I wore little T-shirts and anyone could see I needed a bra.

Lanny's mother kept him home sometimes. We usually didn't ever play in his yard. His mother didn't like it. I guess it wore out the grass. A lot of the people who lived near three-one-two-three Sablain Parkway Drive had those blindsided attitudes. His mother always thought things. People were walking across her grass, kids were playing in her driveway. My mother had a reputation for never coming out and of being a snob. But she didn't care if we played in her yard or even the garage.

When I was fifteen and Lanny nineteen, and the only time we ever did get together, we were sitting on the porch–something I had been doing in order to see him. I would see if Lanny's car was in the drive and if it was I might go sit outside on my porch just in case when he left to go someplace he would see me there. Or sometimes when he came back he would see me sitting outside. And then, not always but sometimes, he would come over and we would sit and talk. Or I remember rainy days when I'd be coming home at lunch time from school and his car would appear and stop and he would say, "Can I give you a ride?" or "Would you and Missy like a ride since it's raining?" But somehow he wasn't really interested in Missy even though she was blond and pretty and knew how to talk. That was the wonderful thing. Somehow because we lived next door to each other he really was interested in me. We shared something just by our proximity I thought. And sometimes he hummed a song while we were riding which was "I'm in the Mood for Love." I don't know if he knew what he was humming.

I had seen him play football–he played center–and graduate and so it was in the summer before I was to enter high school that just before school was due to start he asked one evening when we were sitting on the porch if I'd like to take a walk around the block. It was cold and he lent me his red and white jacket. He was smoking. In spite of all the neighborhood which had a tendency to also sit on the front porches after dinner and look up and down the street, he and I walked around the block and out of sight from everyone and right then he asked me to go to the next football game which happened to be out of town. Such games were off limits for me since I couldn't drive and nobody my age had a car. But I said I'd ask my mother.

I was almost relieved when my mother said no. I would not have been able to hold his interest for an entire evening. I wouldn't have been able to talk. I was convinced that if he knew me he wouldn't like me and so I accepted my mother's answer. I said, "I can't go. My mother won't let me." And probably that was when his mother said, "Don't you ever ask her then again. They think you aren't good enough."

But he did ask again if I would meet him in the drugstore after the next home game.

D and C's Drugstore had been the favorite hang-out for all the school kids. I used to buy my paint sets there and the large India pads. I also got lemon pies that cost eleven cents. It was exactly like what you hear about in the bobby sox days. It used to be so packed with kids that everybody had to stand up like sardines. It was where people met and had dates and danced to a juke box that played things like, "Oh, yes, I'm the Great Pre ten en der." When the football team finished practice there would always be a few of the girls still waiting at D and C's for a ride home. And after a night game, a varsity game, D and C's would remain open to allow people to get a coke, use the phone, dance. That was when I was supposed to meet Lanny.

By the time the game was over I was scared stiff. I had just started tenth grade. I had just come over from Walter French Junior High and had been dating boys with names like Stanley Stover and Marvin Moore who walked me home and held my hand. Of course none of them were to be compared to Lanny.

But now as I pulled open the door to D and C's and looked for him, at first all I could see was a packed house. I looked near the back mirror and I looked around the juke box and then I finally found Lanny way over on one of the stools talking to a girl. I knew if he didn't notice me I wouldn't be able to go over there. It was worse than sitting on the porch and it was far worse than anything. He probably didn't realize that talking to some girl and laughing made it too difficult for me. I couldn't go say "hi". I just stood there and let myself be jostled for a while and then I left.

      ಎ   ಎ   ಎ

Every time I visit my mother I plan what I would do if I lived in her house. I always first of all have the stairway moved into the hall and have the walls knocked down and big windows put in and I take out everything in the living room and put in one overall carpet and have built-in furniture and then I take down the partition between the master bedroom and the den and make one big bedroom and I do the same upstairs where my father tried to make two bedrooms. I just rip it all out and make one decent-sized room and a bath.

The way my father used to work was he'd put up something called beaver board which was soft. You could put your hand through it and in fact I did. He'd tack that up across the studs and then plaster the cracks and paint over the whole thing. Later the beaver board would pull away and the plaster would crack, and the rooms became so crammed with furniture that grandmother left us—one small room had twin beds, a desk, a dresser, a stool, an overstuffed chair, a cedar chest—that after awhile my mother didn't clean it. Who could blame her?

But Sablain Parkway Drive continued on. Some of the same people still live there even now in the 1990s. Some new people moved in. There were, finally, mature trees and driveways and birds in our neighborhood. It was the quietest street in the whole, wide world. People painted their mailboxes and carpeted their front stoops and manicured their lawns. They put up window boxes and decks and awnings

I haven't seen the house Lanny lives in today. Lanny's wife is beautiful, in an Egyptian way. Her eyes look exactly like Cleopatra's, painted on frontwards from the side. Circled in brown. Dark lips. Blond hair. Not at all like me. What was Lanny thinking of? Had he always wanted to marry an Egyptian?

And why did Lanny never go away so that even now when I visit my mother I look out the window toward the driveway or crane my neck for a glimpse of him? Could it be I disliked his round face and stocky body and eventual balding head and still he could be so attractive even with them? What was the problem? Could I be as polite and pleasant as he was? Could I be as even-tempered and kind? What the heck is wrong here? Could I live in the little house?

❧   ❧   ❧

I am not full of charm as Lanny is, nor full of his plainness and goodness. Over the years I've discovered that I can't live in the little houses. I've lived in several different places. For three years I lived in what would be called a monastery on Cape Cod. We had morning prayer, noon prayer, compline, and a hour of prayer in the middle of the night in a chapel. We had to stagger outside winter or summer with a flashlight and pray for whomever or whatever on the prayer list. Sometimes it was cucumbers and sometimes people with cancer and sometimes Richard Nixon.

I've lived on Kirkland Street in Cambridge and was there when Kennedy died. I've heard Marianne Moore read poetry in her tri-corn hat. I've seen Martin Luther King preach in the chapel in Harvard

Yard. I've seen Julia Child in the Somerville grocery when it still had sand sprinkled on the floor, and Al Capp. I lived for a time in a pre-civil war house in Connecticut where I was always finding pieces of dinner ware and jewelry and gravestones on the premises. I attended Yale. I heard Lowell and Tate and Robert Penn Warren and Eugene Waite and Cleanth Brooks and Louis Martz and Harold Bloom.

 I studied Dickinson, attended a class taught by Marie Borroff who began the first session by turning her back to us and writing a quotation on the black board. It said: When the poet's work goes well,/ all the devils scream in hell. But always I returned to my little neighborhood. Always I thought, what if I lived here? How would I remodel the house?

❧   ❧   ❧

 A year or two before I turned fifteen we took Lanny and his brother and parents to the cottage at Wall Lake. That was a rare occasion because the cottage belonged to Grandma and she never let us bring anyone. The lake was sacred to me. Whomever I brought had to pass a test. Sarah Jane had been there just once. Lanny came up, stood around, admired everything. Just the idea of him being there was too much for me. And then, it was a cloudy afternoon, not perfect for swimming. Even so, we got into our suits and we went swimming, the lake warm by now compared to the air. We swam out to the raft, crossing the mucky place. We hauled ourselves up to the raft and lay there. He lay on his back, then on his stomach. I had on my mother's red, two-piece suit. I suppose it was too big for me. I remember I felt it looked okay. We swam back in.

 We liked to run in shallow water. We would run and tag each other and fall in the lake deep enough so it didn't hurt, shallow enough so it was fun. Deep enough so you could go under. And then, he grabbed me–I remember this very well this is something I've remembered for so many years–and held me under the water. I know I was looking up toward the sky and I was not strong enough and I am sure I was under, my cheeks must have been puffed up, because I was holding my breath and my eyebrows were scowling. He held me till I thought I would drown.

 And here is the odd thing. We were sitting at the table after dinner and it was evening. His family was going to spend the night and return the next day which was on a Sunday. All dressed and warm and dry, he suddenly said, "Don't get any ideas now."

In spite of our parents and in spite of the restrictions, clothes, babushkas, midwestern morals, Protestants and Baptists and all the small town thinking, one night when my parents were visiting at a neighbor's he took my sweater away from me and held it behind his back. When I tried to get it he kissed me. When I thought he was done he lifted his lips and then did it again like a postscript, doing it over very gently as if that is what they do–adults. At fifteen, I had thought things like that came single. I remember the date. It was October third.

Years later, when my older brother died, I flew home to Lansing and Lanny came to the visiting hours at Estes-Leadly Funeral Home. It was March but cold and a crust of ice on the sidewalks.

No one else was in the room except some people from the Ramshead (my brother's bar), the minister, and a friend from high school who always comes to these things. And of course there were the relatives and the neighbors. At first, though, there were so few people that we spent our time going up and commenting on the two bunches of flowers. Here were these flowers, here were those: that kind of thing. No one had really expected my brother to die and so it was awkward. No one knew the cause of death. It had been alcohol, but my mother still was telling people he had had the flu. The minister asked 'how nice' I wanted him to be in giving the eulogy for my brother.

"As nice as you can," I said, irritated. "If church's not for this then I don't know what."

"You can mention that he struggled with alcohol and wasn't able to overcome it," I added.

And then Lanny and his white haired father and his brother came in.

❧   ❧   ❧

So it was thirty years later, at my brother's funeral, that Lanny appeared to me again. He was getting a little bald. We stood in a semi-circle with others from high school and talked. He looked good. His brother was there also, much younger and wild looking, like a mountain man. We were trying not to look at the open casket.

We were trying to feel each other out. I remember there was talk of one of the schools and Lanny told me that he and his wife had almost had an accident. They had spun on ice and slammed into a curb.

I sat down on one of those fake suede love seats in funeral parlors. I suppose it was time for him to leave because he was suddenly right there and bent over to say goodbye and then, kissed me. Not full on the mouth but almost. There were whiskers. I was completely taken aback. After thirty-five years five months and four days.

He said, "I'll see you tomorrow", meaning at the funeral, "Sweetie."

Then the mountain man came over, in imitation of his brother, and kissed me too.

Sometimes when I tell this story, I mention things that have happened over the years. Sometimes I speak about finding Sarah Jane again, how she moved back to town after having been a TV producer, and I think about how I was called 'sweetie'. Once in a while, life gives you something back, like the first boy.

I'll Never Leave You

In 1957 when I was finishing my senior year at Everett High, I knew I would not be marrying Kilroy Patchett because I was going to be so famous as a writer in New York and never come back.

He wanted me to live in St. Louis, Michigan, a town next to Paris, and help him run a dairy farm. The equipment necessary for a farm those days cost a million. Kilroy went to Michigan State and he told me we could never get started on our own because we would need, besides a herd of cows, the land and barns and equipment. The equipment was the real expense he said. But his uncle Walter already owned a dairy farm and offered to let him be a partner and this would make it possible; and we could live with him.

Kilroy's Aunt Kitty and Uncle Walter had no children and just the way his aunt read *Redbook*, I could see she was battling temptations: time on her hands, settling down, marrying a second time, maybe even alcohol. But the greatest temptation must have been the pure hot fear she would one day just walk out, take the nearest car or pickup truck, churn down that gravel drive and leave a cloud of smoke. Getting out of a place with one movie house and two dime stores and nothing but black and white cows and Walter couldn't have been that bad.

In the evenings Kilroy told me we'd play pinochle with his Patchett relatives.

Four years before, he gave me a gold cross. I wore it through high school, Humanities l01 and l02 at Michigan State, Honors English, Melville and James, under my cardigan sweater, right up to the time

I was on my own living in Cambridge and playing the guitar in a coffee shop in Harvard Square; and then for some reason I put it away, along with the journalism award Viola Brandt had given me. Mrs. Brandt read *Beowulf* out loud to us while walking up and down the aisles, her knees and ankles creaking like a foreign country. I would have loved to travel to England to the fens and the fogs where Grendel and Beowulf and the men in the great halls slept.

I was given a pin which I put with Kilroy's cross. It was the Betty Crocker Homemaker of Tomorrow award. I never needed the pin, but for some reason I never threw it away.

Kilroy and I went togther for nearly two years in high school. The occasion I chose for breaking up with Kilroy was this. *I'll never forget you,* he wrote in the back of my school yearbook. But the fact that he wrote it seemed to mean that he would forget. Whether I liked him or not, I vowed he was premature. What did he think, disposing of me this way? Where would he go; where was I going? *I'll never forget you?*

He also wrote a mushy letter inside the year book. It spread clear across the page in a flowing hand and it was embarrassing because it thanked me for being generous, when I had been nothing of the kind. As I remember, he said something like, thanks for being so understanding, when actually I had griped at him and complained.

There was a photograph in the yearbook of the entire student body, sophomores, juniors and seniors, in the gymnasium during a basketball game, the referee blowing his whistle on a play, his paunch like a black and white beet, the young man glaring at another one from a folding chair. I can remember him; the kind that shouldn't be there. Everyone else is up in the balcony–I am sitting with friends but Kilroy is not sitting with me because I had decided no more going steady! He is looking down at his lap, his sleeves are rolled up and his shirt is pressed. He looks very tan. He is with a girl named Kay who spells it Kai.

In the book, it says we are going to be married. The teachers all assume it–but what did they know about me? His sister, Toot, calls me, "My sister-in-law-to-be".

It was logical that I would want to see the world and leave him. The end came when I was at Michigan State. I hitched a ride in East

Lansing with a student who turned out to be a Filipino fighter pilot and then we went to the movies. When Kilroy called, my mother told him that I was not at home. When he finally got me, I remember his anguished, *Is this how you're going to end it? Like this?* And it was. I did. Dropped him. Never gave it a thought. Had to be done.

Exactly thirty years later, I had a dream in which Kilroy was so real that I suddenly wanted to try to find my cross. It was hard getting the gold cross untangled from another chain in the jewelry box. The other chain is a locket my husband gave me. The two are all tangled up with a third, silver, chain. At last, I get it.

"What are you doing?" my husband says, hearing me in the bedroom looking for something.

"I've got to keep these separate," I say.

I am surprised at the flip way the story unfolds. I want it to be romantic and deep. I know his arms in the sleeves in the school yearbook were beautiful. And if he were a woman, one of my friends for instance, I could just write and ask, *How are you?*

What if his marriage is gone or he is bald or fat or has no job or is an alcoholic? Or what if he doesn't remember me or he is happily married or what if he is poor? What then?

He used to go into the beer gardens to get his father. His mother worked in a cafeteria at the hospital. *She's high strung,* his mother said about me. His mother had lower incisor teeth which protruded in kind of a pleasing way which made her warm and likeable, and she had a black mustache. But his father was tall and thin. *Stinking drunk!* Kilroy would say about his father. *Drunk as a skunk.*

Darwin and Darlene were the cousins. The family believed in naming from the same initial. I thought it was stupid. I thought playing cards every Saturday night was stupid too. I couldn't bear it.

I imagined that a beer garden was like the place where St. Peter denied the rooster. It would be a courtyard of large paving stones. There would be a Roman arch. Inside, hiding among plants around the perimeter would be Kilroy's father with his back to us looking at whatever it was he saw with his bloodshot eyes.

❧   ❧   ❧

In the dream I got lost–it was a cloudy dream. When I woke I sat directly up in the bed and couldn't think. Usually, when I wake up

I think about the day to come and begin worrying. But this time I felt Kilroy beside me as if the dream had been a visitation.

I put it right out of my mind. This had happened before. I had to clear a path in my mind in order to begin. All that day he was with me but I didn't allow him, tried not to think. But when I took a walk and my mind was not occupied, he seemed to say to me, *"Now you must think."* And I was jittery–I felt as if the sun itself was bending down to look into my face.

It never occurred to me that if I had loved him, I could have tried to make a possibility for happiness. I could have helped him to find a profession and to make a home. But it was so against my nature. When high school was done, I dropped him.

I cannot go back and apologize. Out of guilt you go back, I told myself, and in dreams you search. But I am angry that the dreams come! And for the time that I am searching, I am back sixteen again. *I'll never forget you.* I wonder.

Teenagers have the capacity to be loyal; they are capable of the most amazing acts of gentleness and trust. My aunts and uncles never expected anything else of me. Might not a first love last the life?

I do not mean to sound as if I loved him years later. No, I did not. I had only had the dream again. And this time with a sinking, a terrible sinking revelation. This time there was a choice, and there had never been one there before.

Sometimes I imagine him. I play a game with myself that I find him with his back to me behind a fence on a farm. Doing chores, he turns and recognizes me. I am that kind of woman, it is all in the frivolous. Then I return to my normal life again and leave him again. Other times I am at Wal-Mart looking up and down for food, pizza, ice cream, and pajamas. I am at the cash register to check out, dressed up and having come a long distance. I see him there and he excuses himself from his family to greet me with amazement. He is almost bald and wearing glasses. He will always belong to me. I am that kind of woman.

Even when Kilroy touched me, he tried to be honorable. I could remember only two dishonorable sentences from him, and that in five years. And once when I had the measles he looked at my chest, my "chest" he called it. He was that honorable. And to think I had left the explaining to my mother to do when I left him.

I was in the habit of doing what I intended, and I was going to get out of Lansing. I had to ask myself what I should do about people's feelings. I didn't always empathize, such is the immemorial custom among snobs.

After the name of a piece of land–Virginia–he had dated someone before me. Virginia. And Virginia had been an honors student and had gotten better grades. Neither of us went with him by then but, after the name of a piece of land! Virginia? It was too much.

When he touched me it was as if with a piece of soft flannel, his kiss was so light and brief.

There was a short story about a rose garden and some sisters and a returned soldier and it was like the writing of Nathaniel Hawthorne, dark and discouraging, something hard to grasp in it that if you sucked on it would kill you.

Perhaps this was what I faced. And he might have marten for a collar and silk lining for a hood and, if so, it would look good with his black hair, dark skin and green eyes. And perhaps Virginia has written him? From her excellent prospect?

I would put the old protective crust back on, have no more dreams. Or, I would neutralize the ones I had, either way. It didn't matter. He must go back to the small place he took up in my past. He had grown very large, the more I thought about him.

You could tell him things and he would listen. He was in the world somewhere. Some way, somehow, he had to grow small. I was never alone now. I felt encouraged with him beside me but, he was not there —

ઝ   ઝ   ઝ

After college years, I moved out of Michigan. I had begun to tolerate black and white cows but never regretted losing a dairy farm in St. Louis. Kilroy, I heard, was making wedding dresses for a living in a town farther north. He didn't have a dairy after all.

But in 1957 at the Junior Prom, standing in front of a backdrop made of cardboard, we didn't know all this. We held hands that night for the photographer as young people do, in front of a precipice.

Ernest Hemingway Died

We're sensitive about Hemingway in Michigan. We have the Big Two-Hearted River and we have the summer places and the lake. He was always ours and we appreciated the care he took with his sentences, a parable told to all creative writing classes once the story became known. We knew that Michigan held the spirits of not only Hemingway's stories, his grand stories, but also of the Ojibwa. But Hemingway had been independent, I thought to myself, and somehow he had gotten out of Michigan. Was it because he was a male? What was the decisive moment when a person, male or female, said I'm going to buy a bus ticket and get out of here?

When I began to drive I discovered how surprisingly easy it was. We had a Chevy with fins. I mastered shifting, night, lanes, nerves, going backwards. I learned calm in the face of excitable passengers. Eventually, driving taught me everything I needed to know. It left me alone to make my own choices. A car of one's own is important.

Willy, my father, ought to have known how to make his own choices too because he had a mother who hounded him. I always felt he ought to tell her off but he didn't. He never could.

Nina Mae, my naughty grandmother, would stand at the foot of the table and he should say, "Oh, go to hell." Or when she would say, "My what a nice Mother's Day card this is," and sneer and maybe read the message over. "Must be William didn't read this before he bought and signed it," then he ought to jump up and take it out of her hands. Or when she said that about how soon they were leaving, "Must be you are in a hurry to get home, William." He should say, "Sure the goddamn am!" But he didn't do that. And we came to the cottage so often, every weekend, that the opportunities were endless. In fact, I had never been anywhere else on a vacation.

This particular weekend was cold for July fourth and there were almost no boats out but I liked to be outside and to sit down in private somewhere. Today I went to the raft. It was still on land waiting for the time when it would go out to the swimming area. It had been freshly painted and as I sat on it I could feel the knotholes underneath the paint.

And how embarrassing this was! My grandfather had one of the few rafts on the entire lake and if he saw other kids climbing up on it he would run out on the dock and yell to them to get off, it was private property. It was that kind of a situation. And Grandmother, the same. She was so neat and hard working that she never sat down. And you were better off if she didn't because on the rare times when she did she might start talking about you or your parents or something you cared about.

It was good to be outside away from all the relatives in the cottage. My mother would come out too because she couldn't bear it either. When she did we'd probably get in an argument. I was going to say something about Ernest Hemingway. The papers said it was an accident. I could just imagine the look my mother would make when I debated that. She would get that dark irritated look, as if to shake me out of her head.

Maybe my father, too, with his cigarette, would get free and go out back to smoke. I could probably find him by the garage sitting on a hunk of cement and watching H. George who was my grandfather. There was always something going on out there.

H. George had made many improvements to the cottage. It had a dormitory with windows that opened from floor to ceiling. There was a screened front porch and a long back porch for fishing gear. He had terraced the path from the road to the door. I used to always run down that slope and past the house down to the lake and clear out to the end of the dock when we came to the lake on Friday evenings. The sun would be just going down and the whole grey lake would be getting quiet. I liked to see the night touch it. I liked to wait until there was no light left.

If Willy had to smoke it was better he smoked outside so probably today he was around in the back.

❧   ❧   ❧

"Man I feel lucky to be alive!" Willy said while sitting on a concrete block behind the cottage. He was reading a refrigerator manual.

"—hissing sounds of frost melting." The manual depicted a woman in hip huggers and bell bottoms. Another Annette Funicello.

"Cheese, snacks in the top snack-saver," he read. "In the crisper, lettuce." He read melodically. "Frost-proof. Your refrigerator is protected by this five-year nationwide protection plan."

"Well, that's good to know," my grandfather commented. He was sweeping the cement steps and muttering.

"Yeah baby," said my dad. "I love it. This is how you clean it."

"Hi," I said. "You're around out here."

They didn't answer me. I looked at them for a moment. How still they were really. Not looking at each other. One so young and skinny. My dad was smoking.

"Food preparation tips." my father said. He turned the manual over and looked again at the woman on the cover. She wore heels and a brass studded hip belt. She had a spit curl and dark hair. She twisted around on the refrigerator so that both her shoulder blades rested on it while she looked straight out at the camera. She was wearing what I think of as a pointed sweater.

"Custom Imperial, Willy," my grandfather reminded him. "With a light and a set of panels." He put the broom up and took off his hat and brushed across his forehead. It was white under his hat.

At the beginning of the year he painted all the sections of dock as well as the raft. It was painted grey and there were metal saw horses for holding each section. These had to be carried down to the water and someone had to be the one to take off his shoes and wade into the water and get wet to set the saw horses. I remember that to keep them stable my grandfather would submerge a wooden plank to rest them on.

They were getting ready to do this now. Here it was fourth of July. My father stood up and rolled his pants. He was bow legged and there was a blue vein behind one knee. When you walked behind him you thought his knees would bend and break they were so thin. He had had five hernias. My grandfather was taller and bigger and I only saw his legs once. They were deathly white. When he carried the saw horses he set his jaw, like a trout's.

"Here," he told Willy. "Here, no, here. Ugh!" They were carrying the first saw horses down to the edge of the lake.

"Easy, Willy."

"Wheeeeeew." my dad said setting it down in the sand while the water filled up his footprints.

It was hard to make the planks of wood stay under. The wood might shoot up out of the water under pressure and hit someone. The men went back up on the beach and got two more saw horses. They put them down and tried to line them up evenly with the cottage. My grandfather made all the decisions. They took out the first section of dock.

There were so many things to do at the lake. On Fridays the front porch had to be washed down with hoses. The cushions had to be put out and then on Sunday it all had to be put away again. But it was magic. It was my whole life and soul to be at the lake while the light glinted against water and beech trees and the sound of the waves blew against the shoreline.

They wouldn't let me help them because I was a girl. I was strong. Heck, I was even chubby. I had to prove myself even to let them allow me to bait my hook.

"She's twelve. We have to," they said when I requested the row boat. They knew I knew how to row and swim.

"Naow... their FOLKS let them. We have to." I had heard them talking about me that way. That was perhaps the first time I ever knew I had a life that was in other people's words.

Nina Mae never went outside because she was so busy making cole slaw and sweeping the sand out of the rugs and setting the table. But if company came 'out from Lansing' she might go outside and take a boat ride with them to show them the lake.

My grandfather would hold the boat as it sank down when each person stepped in. He would keep it steady while they teetered to a seat. All this stuff I had been taught. How to move in a boat. But people from Lansing, out for the day, were never used to boats. A sort of pride always came over me watching them file into the boat and my grandfather taking out one of the green camp stools to use in the bow. Nina Mae would get in all but last and he would get in last of all and then they would shove off. He fed the rope around the motor and started it and the boat left on a mirrory streamer. I would shade my eyes as they got smaller until I could just barely count how many people there were, low in the water and vulnerable.

My grandma was saying something now. It was so windy I couldn't hear it. She scowled into the light. She tried again. Whatever it was, she was saying it under the changing conditions of the wind.

"Would you like to ... eat ... before you ... leave?   William says ... you are ... leaving."

So he was inside.

The table was set. Today there were nineteen because my aunt's and uncle's families were there. I saw my dad all hunched-up in a corner. He looked helpless. He couldn't leave as long as Nina Mae went through the motions of preparing the food and setting it out. He couldn't decently leave right after dinner either. That was understood.

Nina Mae's green eyes were made of liquid and drew into points where her glasses clamped. "You said, 'coffee?'" she asked him.

"Huh," he said.

We all faced forward trying not to notice. Nina Mae's coffee cup was made of pink plastic and she had gold clips to snare her white hair. Altogether she made a pastel sight. My dad was dark with black hair and hazel eyes and an English nose and high forehead. His pants were rolled back down and he had his shoes and socks on.

Suddenly he drew out a cigarette. This made us all draw a breath. "William's done eatin'."

She filled another cup with coffee.

"You just got here," she observed.

"Nope," he said not looking at her. He was mad. His mouth was drawn into a pout. His eyes were just like hers, green and wet. He was correct, we had been here all weekend. Now was the time to tell her to leave him alone but, he got up and headed for the stairs to the dorm.

"When you come back, you might as well bring our coats," my mother said.

Nobody else said anything. My grandfather took the tip of my cousin's hair and made a pencil out of it to tickle her with. When my dad came back he had the wrong coats.

"William, those aren't even ours," my mother said.

Her eyes looked sad and small.

"Seems like you is always in a hurry, William," my grandma said.

"No," he said.

He backed out of the room, tipping over a chair.

"A family shouldn't be like this," my mother said, quivering. My brother Donnie and I looked from one to the other.

"Get your things," my mother said to us, unpleasantly.

❧   ❧   ❧

If my dad had given me any fact about life it was this suffering and his willingness to do it. I would have just chucked the whole thing. I felt sick about it. On the ride home we passed the Wishing Tree. It had been cut way down and not very many people knew it was a wishing tree anymore but I would always wish on it when we left the lake. And the thing I would wish for was that I could go to the lake soon again. Which was silly because I always did, the very next weekend.

And it was silly because that was where my brother had drowned and where my parents had tipped over in the sail boat and my mother got her ankle caught and it was where all this other stuff happened.

But even in school during the winter I used to go over to the window and look out and wish I were at the lake.

"Why is Grandma like that?" I asked sometimes of my mother.

"She just is. She didn't want him to get married. She didn't want him to leave her."

"But why? Why?"

"Because she doesn't know what else to do."

Finally, when my dad lost his health, when his lung collapsed and she could still walk faster than he could to any door and heave it open and hold it for him who walked bent over to protect his groin, then he would cling to a wall sometimes and wheeze to get his breath to try and tell her that he was angry. That was when I wanted to force him to say it. I wanted him to choose away from Nina Mae and FOR my mother. I could see that he should and that otherwise he would die and not do it. But one day it occurred to me that as they said in church, this was his cross. He carried it all stooped over and I was glad it was not my cross and I would not have carried it. I hope I would have if it had belonged to me. All the same, I doubt I would have.

"William, I am going to leave you the money in the will," my grandmother told him. She meant she was leaving it to him and not to my mother.

"Then you can keep your damn money," he told her gasping. "You just keep it. We don't need it. We've never needed it or any other thing you've tried to give us."

His blood pressure was high, but he kept control of himself. My grandmother was playing solitaire on the coffee table. That's what he told me. All the while she was talking she had the cards. She wanted him to visit more often, she wanted to control. My father was so angry he stood up and went out the door and came home and he and my mother went into the bedroom and talked. And in there they began to disagree with each other.

Today however at the lake as we were leaving it was my turn to write in the cottage log-book: I wrote: "Fourth of July. Clear and cold! Ernest Hemingway died."

And Donnie my brother signed his name under mine in his shaky hand. Then we turned through the pages and found all kinds of messages that people wrote–bits of wisdom, weather, corny poems, fishing advice.

And someone had signed it in Hawaiian–probably someone from the church in Lansing–in this foreign tongue, and underneath it was translated.

LANO	MAE	YUR	LUM	REEK
(beautiful spot	warm water	good fishing	fine people)	

Marie-Cone

These were difficult times. My naughty grandmother was completely bedridden. She hadn't eaten much for days and, except for Marie-Cone, was totally alone. My grandmother was definitely reaching the end of a long life. It was shocking to see the way she looked, to find her lying down all the time. Even so, there were some funny moments.

Marie-Cone was determined to finish the relationship with no hard feelings but she had had a twenty-year non-speaking period with my grandmother. No one blamed Marie Cone for it certainly. My grandmother was notorious. In fact the earliest memories I have are of her antics if they may be called such. At that time we lived only a few blocks away from her and a few blocks were not far enough.

Of the things I remember most about her in those early days these are a few: she would call my mother while my father was at work and talk to her for up to an hour and a half. I would hear my mother's 'un-huh, un-huh,' and sense her increasing frustration. These one-sided conversations ended with my mother in tears. But my mother always tried reason first, logic, kindness, firmness, and then the last option. Meanwhile, I got into things. I took out the entire contents of my father's desk while my mother motioned for me to keep quiet. Or I went outside and rang the doorbell. Later, it was my brother who was allowed free range while she talked. I remember wondering why my mother couldn't get many words in. At home she had plenty to say.

Another item connected with my grandmother was her unbending cleanliness. She subjected us to tales of her cleaning which went beyond bounds. My grandmother cleaned the insides of all her cabinets according to a monthly schedule, something we never did. Words cannot express the things my grandmother cleaned and felt needed to be cleaned, but one time, to mention one of these, I painted a picture in oils of the cottage at Wall Lake and gave it to her for Christmas. She liked the painting, it was positively thick with paint but I was happy with it: she was hard to please. But the first thing she wanted to know was 'How do I clean it?'

Another thing about her was her desire to see my parents, but probably this meant her son, my father, at least every Sunday. Thus, we met at her house for every holiday including Father's Day, Mother's Day, and Memorial Day/Labor Day plus every birthday in the family. And, as time went on, my father's brother, Uncle Robert, had five children which added substantially to the list. Nevertheless, we got together for every single one.

My grandma quizzed me about what we had done with things she had given us. Do you still have that doll I gave you? I thought you'd have lost it by now. This always put me in a fierce bad mood. Furthermore, my grandma bordered on paranoia. Determined to be as good as other people, which her own childhood had predisposed her to fearing she wouldn't achieve, she now spent most of her time thinking that people found her falling short and the rest of the time finding fault with what they did. This made for uncomfortable conversations and encounters with people not in the family.

The list of people who did not do as my grandma wanted stretched wide and as I said for a time included even her sister, Marie-Cone. I know it included me. At one time, my mother said that my grandma was about to cross anyone off her list who didn't write back to her but that would have burned so many bridges that in the end she did not go quite that far. For years, my brother Don who was in the Navy was on her 'out' list but then he died a few weeks before she did and she couldn't condone such detachment in herself toward one of her own.

That Marie-Cone would do everything humanly possible to take care of my grandma in the way that she would like is understandable, the idea being that perhaps this time she could continue until Grandma died, at which point we could all relax. But once the relationship was occurring, getting along with my grandmother turned out to be almost more difficult than she could endure. I had found this to be true also.

With Marie-Cone my grandmother would suddenly start behaving in a less than reasonable way. She might have been fine with me five minutes previous (not having seen me for a year because I lived in the Northeast) and then when Marie-Cone came she might argue over what kind of bristles the brush had. It was very hard for Marie.

My grandma might request a certain kind of prescription to be filled and Marie would say that she would go do it immediately. Then my grandma would say, "And get the full prescription, get enough."

Then Marie would say, "No, Nina. They go bad." Then my grandma would counter with, "Well, I don't know anything anymore."

That was a very uncharacteristic thing for her to say–that she didn't know anything–and so then Marie would tell me privately that Nina is not herself anymore at all. Marie-Cone would wear a death dealing look on her face when she said it because nothing could be worse than imagining life without Nina. Nothing could be more difficult or impossible to imagine than life without daily, twice daily, phone calls.

Another odd thing about all of this was that my grandmother was beautiful. She had the kind of face even when she was fifty and sixty which stopped traffic. Her eyes were oval and green and large, her complexion was peaches and cream, her mouth like a rosebud my mother used to say and her teeth like little pearls. And that was the way of it. She continued to look this way for several more decades. But Marie-Cone, although she was a half sister, and close relation, had sallow skin, murky eyes, salt and pepper hair and a certain concentrated worry which made her scowl. My grandmother was always beautiful and Marie was exactly like her in features but somehow not beautiful.

꙳   ꙳   ꙳

A few days before my grandmother died I was visiting in town to attend the funeral of my brother, Don. And so of course I wanted to visit my grandmother. When I arrived at the huge and expensive building for the elderly, I found Nina lying on her side in the bed, moaning, and Marie-Cone not there yet. I immediately knelt at the side of the bed, sat on the carpet, and found myself looking up into the mouth of my grandmother. I had never seen her like this, never without her teeth looking white and polished and straight with their gold bracelets. Now here suddenly it seemed as if the teeth had tumbled together, fallen down. Nothing looked straight. Her forehead was creased and she wasn't sounding right either. There was a definite wheeze. She also was hiding something under her pillow.

I took one of her hands, very gnarled by now. She turned toward me, her hair a fright. The white hair that looked so lovely all the time, so like a cloud, was not anything but tags and rags.

Now Marie was coming, but before she did, I got in a few words at least. I told her I was here. I, at least, was here and holding her, my grandmother, the one I had had for fifty years.

When Marie-Cone came in, I still had hold of my grandmother's hands. I was still even kneeling. Marie-Cone's mouth was pursed the way it always did, involving her nose and forehead. She and Nina. "Two peas in a pod" my mother said. "Of course, not in the SAME pod," she said. By that she meant that they had different fathers. "Two peas in a pod otherwise," my mother said.

Marie-Cone was wearing small shoe boots that zipped. It had snowed last night as it always does in Lansing in March and indeed Marie had had to shovel herself out.

"I got here fast," she couldn't help saying.

My grandmother's room had a powder blue bedroom rug. Actually, the bedroom was the whole apartment except for the bathroom. Since she had been moved into a fancy Life-Care Facility, she had by stages been induced to 'come down' to just one room. There were still things in the storage closet downstairs which she wanted. Up until recently my visits to my grandmother always involved going to the storage deposit area where she would take a key and check on things. It was horrifying to see the old stuffed owl which had adorned the cottage at Wall Lake. It was scary seeing the clocks and photographs and vases without their support systems. But there they were and the idea was to give me something. Of course since I had come by plane, my ability to take anything back was limited.

My grandmother would also want me to eat with her in the dining room. She was however not an adventurous eater and she had the quirks of her practicality. For one thing, she covered her coffee cup as soon as it was poured with a plastic plate which was part of a child's dish set. That was to keep it warm and signal the waitress not to add any liquid. She gave me one of these dishes. Also, she was extremely suspicious of the food and, because of that, she had snacks in her room as well, Little Debby cakes and crackers. She wanted to be able to serve something when one of her grandchildren visited.

What was left of her furniture (from two houses) was in that single room and she could tell to the inch how much space everything took. My grandmother had lived in a large old house on the old side of Lansing by the Fisher Body Plant and the factories. And she had always had a cottage for the summer. When those two residences were sold she and my grandfather had moved into a trailer but it was a large, luxurious one. Her recent move to the Life Care Facility had been necessitated by the death of my grandfather and her own loss of a driver's license.

Even here my grandmother was a dainty and immaculate housekeeper. A formidable housekeeper.

"Did you have to shovel out?" she asked Marie.

"Yes," she said. "Ernie couldn't help me. I didn't dare let him out." (Ernie had Alzheimer's.)

"My glasses, my glasses. Where are they?"

"Here, Nina," said Marie. "Right here on this arm."

There was a metal table on wheels right by her bed. This was where she had her water glass. I noticed that now the only way she drank was through a straw. And her pills were up there. There was a wastebasket directly beneath. A walker too was in the room. Since it was hard to get around my grandmother was developing the tendency to secrete items within arm's reach. The thing she had hidden under her pillow was her hairbrush. Nobody was going to get that. Once when she lived in a slightly larger apartment at the Life Care Facility, the staff recommended a raised toilet seat. "When you go, you can take it along," they added.

"Where I'm going you don't need these," she had replied.

Arthur Halsey was Nina's father, alone, but both Marie and Nina had had the same mother, Maggie Horne. Maggie was a fat woman who lay in bed beneath a parrot. I know that because I was there once as a child and I remember we couldn't move her to change her bed. We had to wait until a few more men came out to help. It took three men to move Maggie Horne is what I heard. But Arthur Halsey had been something else. He had managed to live with a certain independent charm in the country. His second wife was saintly and good, and deaf. Arthur collected arrowheads and tended gypsy moth traps. He was an intelligent, shrewd old man and between Maggie and him, I liked him best.

"Nina," Marie said. "Have you taken your medicine?"

"I think I dropped it in the wastebasket," my grandmother replied.

Marie-Cone always talked between clenched teeth. This was rather pleasing. But she looked to me at that moment as if she had high blood pressure. Her face was flushed and her eyes were bright. She had shoveled herself out of the driveway because her husband would have forgotten and walked off and gotten lost. Or he might have gone outside in his underwear.

Nina and Marie used to ride in the car with him but Ernie Cone wouldn't let them turn on the air conditioning even if it were summer and ninety. He retained sole authority in the car right up until the day they knew they couldn't let him drive it anymore, right up until the day they had to direct him right and left to get home. "It must have been quite something to have been a fly on the wall in that car," my mother said, "before they wrested control away from Ernie."

"I spoke to the doctor yesterday," Marie-Cone said to me in a whisper. "It is hard getting to see the medical people here. She pays so much money and then with all of this what does she get?"

It was plain to see that Marie was exhausted, trying to get answers about Nina's condition. The doctors were saying that she only had the flu, but it was apparent to me that Nina was failing. Furthermore, Marie-Cone, hampered by a basic lack of understanding where medical matters were concerned, was having to fly blind. Determined to get the best care for my grandmother, at the moment, the best care seemed to revolve, for her, around the bottles of pills. Would my grandmother take the pills for pernicious anemia, and for her heart, and the ones for blood pressure?

Marie-Cone wanted my grandmother admitted into the hospital facility. And a further hurdle for today–and it was a big one–was how to get my grandmother ready to visit her doctor. It was going to be necessary for my grandmother to be dressed and ready in time for the wheelchair crew at ten o'clock this morning, to take her down to the lobby in the elevator, and put her on a Health-Care van for transporting to the doctor's office. Of course, Marie-Cone was going along.

It appeared, however, that my grandmother had either lost all interest in eating or was determined to die. Since she was eighty-five, very weak, and suffering from many ailments, I thought this was a more subtle issue than Marie-Cone did. But Marie-Cone did not want Nina to die whatever happened.

"Ohhh, I am so tired. I don't feel good. I am going to sleep."

"No, you're not, Nina!"

Nina had just finished giving me a gift from her built-in closet. She had not been able to get up and show me its contents but she had directed me with words. I had not worn boots this morning. I needed boots. Would I like some? She had an extra pair in her closet. I must take them. In her closet I found a pair very like Marie's. We had just made that transfer of goods when Marie came in.

"Nina, I can't see here the pills you are supposed to take," Marie said lifting each plastic container and trying to read the labels. "What do you suppose has happened?"

"Oh, I don't know . . . did they drop down?"

"Oh, Nina. You mean they went into the wastebasket?" looking angrily at me. "Then we must find them." She searched hard in the basket. She didn't find them. There ensued a discussion between them as to whether the cleaning people threw out the pills. It was resolved by Marie-Cone's decision to question the cleaning staff at length.

"Well, Nina, we've got to get you ready to go downstairs," she said, giving up on the one issue and bracing herself for a new one. "Do you need to go to the bathroom?"

"No, I don't need to."

"Nina, you'd better go."

"No, I'm okay."

"Nina. You need to go to the bathroom first."

My grandmother got up on one elbow. Evidently things became dizzy. She looked wildly around her.

The bathroom was directly across from her bed, probably ten feet away. I could see into it. The door was open. It had an especially wide door for wheelchairs. My grandmother got herself sitting up, facing it. She looked wildly at it, her hair standing up every which way, very unlike her Eastern Star hairdo. Marie-Cone brought the walker to her. I was still kneeling by the bed.

"Oh dear," said my grandmother. "Oh dear." She stood up and started with the walker toward the door. She was very unsteady. "Oh dear oh dear oh dear oh dear."

I was reminded of my own self-admonitions when I heard her. These occurred at such times as exam time. "I'm not turning out right," I said at these times. "Oh, dear. I'm not turning out. Nobody likes me. I guess I can't make it. Oh, dear."

"Oh dear," she continued and got into the bathroom.

We heard her tinkle and then she reappeared. And there was a knock on the door that startled us all. It was the ambulance driver. He was fifteen minutes early. This irritated Marie-Cone no end. Now we had to get a coat on her and get her down the hall and into the elevator before she was ready.

"The kind of service they have here," hissed Marie to me, "is disgraceful. They've sent the driver half an hour too early. How are we supposed to handle that?"

Eventually, my grandmother and Marie and I got into a huge long elevator. We all faced forward. My grandmother had that deep furrow between her eyes. Her hair was a sight. Marie-Cone on the other hand was dressed all in beige. She wore a wool hat and scarf and coat. She was bundled and buttoned up tight. Here was Marie-Cone about to have a heart attack and here was my grandmother with her hair sticking up and here was I seeing my grandmother for the last time.

"Where is my brush? Do you have it?"

Marie-Cone gave me a wild look. We'd both seen it under Nina's pillow but we hadn't remembered it. "Do you have the brush, Marie?" She was getting querulous.

"No," I said quickly. "We don't have it right now."

So Nina took her hands and patted her hair down. Marie-Cone looked even more miserable.

When we wheeled her into the lobby–a huge mauve and teal place where everything matched and a large rose pattern covered the walls and rugs–there were people all over and the lobby had a quiet, fawning kind of feeling. Forced cheer advertised itself on bulletin board and poster.

We wheeled her outside to the curb where the van was already idling. How cold it was! The van had an automatic door and tracks that lowered so that we could roll my grandmother on.

She sat waiting on the wheelchair like some kind of white-haired gorilla all hunched over, perched on tracks in the back of the van. Then Marie-Cone climbed up in front with the driver and that was the way they went to the doctor.

I waved. I was feeling very emotional. I had hugged her, told her I loved her. It was serious but now even my grandmother seemed to sense the incongruity. This was certainly an odd way to travel! Well, it was. Here was I her oldest grandchild. And here she was. She looked sheepish. It's come to this I supposed she was thinking. Here I go, alone in the back of a van with my hair a mess and your grandfather not even knowing all this. She might have remembered what I said to her earlier. In order to calm her anxieties of which she had as many as Marie-Cone, I had told her she had left a beautiful family. "They are a beautiful family," I said. "Sure, they are scattered all over but they are healthy and they are good people. You can relax." (If it wasn't true, I couldn't help it. At that moment I thought she ought to let the little issues go. I could even see her eyes relax.) So now she waved, sheepishly, but somewhat pleasantly, in the old style. I thought it might be the last time. Marie-Cone waved too, grimly, and that was how I said my last words.

Earlier, we had talked briefly about my brother's death. My grandma kept saying, "Now write it down that Donnie has died or by tomorrow I won't remember it." But she did remember it. When I got there she wanted to know where he was going to be buried.

"Was it over on the right by the Newths? or was it further by the baby cemetery (where my brother Doug had been buried so long ago, and where I am sure they would not put a grown man like Donnie) or was it by the—and here she took a deep breath—the Messengers?" (My mother's family, God forbid!)

I said I would see.

The Reindeer Boy

> — *The cell is the fundamental unit of life. It does everything that is characteristic of life which is to say it replicates, grows, metabolizes. It is the smallest unit that can do those things. And what does the liver do? It does everything. It is a vicious and depraved organ.*
> — from a college physiology text.

This is how my mother described my brother Don in the hospital.

He was in withdrawal the day he arrived. They wanted to regulate his fluids, so they gave him no liquid. They let him suck on ice. He wanted a glass of water. He told me to call a taxi and he would leave. He thought that I would. I did not, however. He was surprised at me. He began to rave.

They inserted a needle directly into the stomach cavity and suctioned it. They drew off eight liters. Then his stomach softened and his eyes grew smaller, although they still looked engorged. However, his hands appeared less pudgy. He has such fat fingers, I had exclaimed to you. He has such fat hands!

They would not consider placing him on a kidney machine and why was that? Clearly, his kidneys were not handling fluids. He was struggling to breathe. They put him on a respirator. (He had been in intensive care two weeks by that time but the time went by fast.) How peaceful he looked! We were thinking, your sister and I, how peaceful he looked.

You, on the East Coast, sent him a letter. "Read it to him," you said. "It will tell him how I feel." But we didn't read it. Not right away. Maybe tomorrow. "Please read the letter," you finally said, but by that time he wasn't talking. Nothing more than a nod, or a groan. He was listening, the nurse said. "Maybe he can hear us." He is sleeping peacefully, she said. Was he in a coma? Was he listening or not? I wanted to read the letter then. We better not wait because there was no time.

His liver was not functioning. Was it the color of blue violet? Still, his heart was strong and I argued for that. Look there he lies I said to the doctor. Breathing, sleeping, peaceful. I think he hears us. I'd like to get him into a treatment program. If he'd let me. We'd discussed which one, one daughter and I. But, said the doctor, at the level of the cell, the doctor said, what of that? Fluids were not passing to and fro, I said, from the plasma, membrane to membrane separating the slippery transit from organs, and the membrane–that delicate stitch of life that staves off disaster–that was working wasn't it?

ਃ   ਃ   ਃ

Before this we had to take his cat, Worthless, to the vet to be put to sleep. She was a cat he'd picked up in Bermuda. He had nothing there but the little apartment and the yard, the ocean, and that cat. She was a tortoise shell with yellow eyes and a black line running along her nose. She was his pride and joy, the only thing he loved, the only thing he had left.

He was gone most of the day but when he came home he would pay attention to that cat, get her cans of food, hold her, pet her and take her outside in the recliner to watch the ocean. After he moved home of course he brought the cat, moved home with all the packing boxes and set them up unopened in the basement since he would be moving out.

Worthless wouldn't pay any attention to anyone else at first. She waited for him. He doted on her. Finally, after she had been with us a year, she decided I knew how to feed her as well. And then she started snuggling up on my robe in my lap. But, she would not come into other rooms. To stay in the kitchen on the one chair nearest the heat was enough for her. Perhaps Bermuda had been like that–a chair by the wall and the chattering of squirrels. I gave her food and let her drink out of the faucet. After a time she came, a year I say, to sit upon my lap when I wore my robe in the evening. She was a big hunter. The neighbors complained that she killed a bird. It'd be Don's cat they said to each other. Worthless. How ridiculous was that. All the animals in the neighborhood and it's got to be Don's cat. But I couldn't keep her in. She also prowled around in the basement among the crates that were filled with his cooking utensils, TV, his Navy photographs.

Yes, if something went wrong in the neighborhood–a dead squirrel–they blamed this cat but all it wanted was a life for itself, nothing but the deserved things. "Having lost my children," he said, "you'd think I could at least keep one cat." (I thought of the documents upstairs, unopened, owed child support, the unopened bank statements.)

It seemed a pretty tie to me: the way they got along. He and the cat didn't seem to take much interest in any other. The sum was not large, so to speak, compared to other sums, but to them it seemed large–the two together. And that was all. "Could they not possibly keep me a little longer?" the cat might have said but that came after. Where Worthless used to press her eye, beside the door, held me for hours. The number of times I have said that word 'Worthless' whenever I want to let her in.

We must have spoken to Dr. Weir about her around six o'clock. In general appearance I felt the cat was sick, longed for an empty place close and warm with artificial light if need be. Otherwise no preference. In the days that followed we visited several veterinary lodgings without much success. They usually said it was no easy matter with the cat and I couldn't come to an agreement with any of them.

Finally, I found a basement box and put some old rags in and Worthless would lie there when I was gone, but otherwise would prefer my lap. "You would think I could at least keep one cat." I understood.

I never put her out in bad weather and hoped to nurse her along. Without the cat I didn't know how he was to survive. He was comfortable enough as long as the cat would stay. He didn't find a job. He was always looking for the mail. I didn't see much coming. But certain evenings when the weather was fine and we felt equal to it, we fetched a chair and sat looking at the sky. What lacerated him was her sickness.

Dr Weir would gladly procure another for us or advance her death, he said. That was kind. Unfortunately, we did not need to advance her death.

I tried to get her to suck without much success. Her mouth was covered with milk. The milk fell to the floor and was lost. Little by the little it had the power to stir my heart. Things were getting worse.

Just to know it had a being however faint was enough for me; it was as bad as that. Neither Don nor I wanted to do anything. I'd look at that stripe down her nose and try to see if she were breathing. And came the moment the vessels stopped communicating, you know, the vessels. I know, but all the same. Worthless, with the eyes of a flame as if a child set a match to it and the strange line almost center, but not quite, on her nose. It meant to go straight but without the certainty, do you see what I mean?

So I left the windows down the way when a moth is caught you don't want it to fly in. You want it to go out. I can't explain. One thing, at least in an hour it would be too late. In a half hour.

I thought, for the moment, I'm here, I will wait. All ears. Tired out.

I haven't answered where we buried her, where we buried the cat. All I know is, don't offer to bring me another because I wouldn't want it unless it be that one.

        ა   ა   ა

Right after, he got sick. I knew he'd put on too much weight. I could hardly find clothes for him. But how it happened he was home at all, how he wrote and said he needed to come immediately—only he didn't put it that way—he asked me at the end of a letter might he come up to Michigan to pay me a visit—well, I felt I'd caught sight of my son after all those years. I saw him striding along almost certain to get a job. He'd been a Navy Chief. And he'd done well. We read the letters of commendation. Oh, he had his faults. But there were letters. He couldn't mow the lawn he was so fat. He begged me to let him mow the lawn and then it winded him. What's wrong with you, I might have said, but didn't. And so he stayed two years before the first thing happened.

What happened was that he hit the flu season. I personally could not tell, but it was winter, late February and I thought it was the flu. He told me we'd have to call the doctor the next day. But when the day came he said, "Let's see if we can hold out a little longer." Nothing happened after that until a bit later. He couldn't get up the stairs to bed. He started sleeping in the chair in the living room. I tried to lend a hand by lifting him up to ease his back. He had used to slip out of his sponge slippers when he came in, late afternoons, from the Rams Head. Slip into his little plastic slippers and go upstairs and take a nap. I wouldn't see him again until supper time.

But now it was obvious that something was wrong. He'd stopped eating the chips and pizza at midnight. He was very pale. I found a letter to a doctor he'd written which made me think he'd known something a long time.

"Would you like for me to call a doctor?"

"Let's wait another day," is what he said. "And then I'll let you call an ambulance."

"You don't need an ambulance surely!" I croaked. "I'm capable of driving you." But, no, he said. An ambulance. Finally, the day came when he said: call it. I remember he was lying in the lounge chair. He had gotten the new car, a Crown Vic eight cylinder four door. He was proud of it. He needed one in order to look for a job. He had had the automatic windows fixed.

ஐ ஐ ஐ

When the aid opened the curtains the sun blasted in his eyes. He almost squinted. The nurse pulled away his clothes to reveal his left nipple as one does for someone who has dropped dead. But he was stiff and fully closed his eyes. Through the windows we caught a glimpse of nothing except the sky out the seventh story window and a plane probably on a domestic flight, but he began to breathe heavily so a nurse stopped a third time, of her own free will, and, crammed with pills and things upon a tray, said, "Where to?"

Such stiffness of the lower limbs. She bent his left leg. Back and forth. He did not open his eyes. There was a flabby old piece of flesh, the other leg tossing wildly, and then he gave an unpredictable jolt of the pelvis. She informed me that he must flex his knees. For what? I wondered, but it always ended in the same way. Nobody answered.

He looked sore and mistrustful. I recalled that he had always been an easy child to raise, in love with story-telling and wild tales. His fabrications, his prancing under the furniture pretending he was a reindeer with you. You both played Christmas reindeer: you called him the Reindeer Boy. You would go to the forests to seek for food and would enter the stag forest under the dining table or behind the chairs. The reindeer fixed their hands in the shape of hooves.

The nurses aids were acting as though we were going to a fair. "No need for them to use caution," I thought. The weather was fine. The floor was full of vehicles and they came our way with great speed. A janitor with a cart stopped-in and said he broke his femur I think. That might have been what he said or it might have been something else. It might have been the bit of Old Testament we tried to keep from entering the room.

The nurses aids as I say were fixing for a party. When it came time for me to look at the record, I couldn't read it. From time to time they brought food, but it was not for him. From time to time they were looking for things around him. But why I did not know.

"Sign here on the bottom line," they had said when he was first admitted. He played with the pen but wouldn't sign it. I think he thought it might have been a trick. And why should he agree to it, if it were? "You could have signed it," I said when they had gone. "Nope," he answered me.

They brought a stretcher and he lay down on it. They inserted the tubes. They hooked him up. "Where can I reach you," he said to me going down the hall past anonymous ruins, "if necessary?"

There were times he looked alert. He was redder than ever, in the face. He had lost his slippers. I wanted to know if they were there in the little cupboard beside the bed. He asked for a drink of cold water but they would not give it. Even on the bed-side table the glass had to be removed. About three o'clock he roused and set off again asking for it. We figured withdrawal. He couldn't have his cigarettes.

He had underlined the addresses of some people for me to call. They were people from the Rams Head. He marked some with a cross for me to try and contact but it proved fruitless because no one was at home and, as I hate to call the Rams Head itself, there was no success. He ruled out some names with a diagonal stroke. Later, he showed me another paper. I was supposed to contact those.

His hands and fingers were as fat as sausage, his sister said. He begged me to call the last address in his book and I promised to. It was a woman named Clarice. He might have winked. Or winced when I said it. I did reach her or, that is, I left a message.

He had neither eaten nor drunk for three days. I mentioned this to the aide who replied that he could have no liquid or food until things were back to normal. She was very serious about that. Nevertheless, I saw clearly that his eyes were closed, his hands flat on the rough cover of his bed and that he had given up all efforts to extricate himself. I would have liked an open eye, even a movement of hand, but then maybe he wouldn't have been able to handle it after all this.

I thought, no reason for this to go on and on. Then let it end. But the efforts of the kidneys and liver and working of the heart with all that fluid, the breath in his nostrils, the feet higher than the head and of course you had written one of your letters, and could we read?

I saw he was resting easily. Once I thought he might rise but it was an illusion. He liked to tell stories but you know. Of no consequence, it came to me, that once upon a time he had had a dog, a black weenie, extremely sleek, that ran away often into the woods by slipping its collar. Whenever we found him, wet and panting heavily, he would be down near the monkey trails and the sewer pipes.

It was at this point Clarice came, from the Rams Head. I don't know whether she worked there. She was a sturdy shape and wore a flowered dress off the shoulders believe me as if she were leaving for a cruise that very day. She cried oh how she cried and took his hands and told him to his face, that they would travel and what she saw was a lonely man. He looked at her only. The thought came to me cruelly that she would get no more out of him.

Then everyone was gone. His silence seemed natural now, though he was naturally garrulous and used to speak first. I resolved to speak, nevertheless, to him. I opened my mouth thinking I would hear the words, but I heard a kind of rattle, mere speechlessness due to long silence.

Another visitor came in, Tony. He stopped there speechless halfway in as if to go right up and then thought better of it and stopped back, beside me, and finally backstepping as if downhill, although of course it wasn't.

This Tony I knew my son must have entertained with his stories and now Tony turned, I mean half wheeled in a semi-circle not being able to start forward again, and said, "I didn't know it was this," but also saying, "Can the man speak? I thought it was just the flu."

He has been gathering fluids for years, the doctor said. I could assent to this, and so could Tony. I thought about the smell of his aftershave in the bathroom, mixed with something I couldn't place. The burned cocoon marks in the carpet by his bed. And the unaccounted-for pitcher of water. To pour upon the fires? The absence of ashtray. The accumulation of thousands of Q-tips. And then, too, the letters we all sent him over the years, along with his bank statements and advertisements.

His Navy dress blues hanging on a coat rack, with four gold hash marks on the sleeve. There was never any career but the one at seventeen against our wishes. Now just memories put under our feet, the city of his childhood.

But here was a strange thing. I saw a lush pasture and those white cabbage moths, and his white-blond curls as a baby so fuzzy it was as if he were a sheep. And beyond this meadow to my certain knowledge there was a path and he upon it. Such was the scene.

We needed a story at this point. One of your stories, something like that. Or the one about the shark in the basement, or the one about the boat he always told everyone his father was building down there, out of sheer imagination. He might have simply told that story, but he was asleep. He knew the story by heart. So did I.

Would that have calmed us? I dozed off. He skipped a beat. I crossed the meadow of those white moths again with little stiff steps. The best I could manage. No trace of where we had been when he was young. His small footprints. Having need of air, his bruised lids opened. My heart in my breast and then a sound. Like a hoot. But he could not talk or answer.

"The further the tube goes the longer the tube stays in," they told me.

I thought we might get him to an alcohol treatment place. He turned quickly or seemed to. I waited, sitting on a kind of chair beside his bed. As to what hour it might have been I have no idea.

"What's the matter?" he might have said to me, distinctly, although he couldn't have. Not with the tube.

But by now the kidneys were paid out, and his fingers closed. It's no use rushing matters; things will cease anyhow gently as they can. Little by little, like falling asleep. I could see in spite of everything, he was doing that.

I could hear the traffic, the little bell that summoned nurses. But he did not open his eyes and ring the bell for the ice again. It was as if he might have unlit the lamps. I asked him, sometime that night, by way of conversation, if I might light the lamps, but I knew the answer.

The Dreams of My Mother

In the last days I had to travel to Michigan because that's where I'd left my mother, an old woman who didn't cut her hair and was an alcoholic.

Michigan is unfortunate as a state–great lumber potential and then Henry Ford developed an automobile. When I arrived the mass exodus to Tennessee was occurring. You couldn't buy a trailer or a car. Sixty-two thousand high school graduates were out looking for jobs. People were leaving for states where there weren't any unions as fast as they could pack. Poles and Finns. The Detroit River burned day and night with the fever to leave. There was so much garbage in the streets you thought you were in another country.

When I'd lived there, back in the fifties, it was a state devoted to football and stern German virtues. As college students we aspired to jobs in marketing or hotel management, the era of agriculture being finished. We'd never heard of hypodermic needles then, or HIV.

Now, the state seems closed up. You can walk the main streets of Lansing and never see a soul. The Capitol building, the R. E. Olds and Body-by-Fisher factories, tool and die–all dead. Libraries are closed. The school system has failed.

My mother, too, was trapped. What could an old woman in a tiny house between two massive highways, with liquor stores tended by Vietnamese, do? She didn't even have the Olds Ciera anymore. She'd backed it into an insurance salesman at a Party Shoppe. But what I'm telling about is how I came to be arriving thirty years later.

She was so weak, she couldn't get up to walk or let me in. I had to use the back door which wasn't locked. I crept in following the sound of music playing too loud to find her in the bedroom. There was my mother like a zombee in her own bed listening to country and western! I was amazed how emaciated she was and how she'd let herself get into this condition. I have never seen anything so awful. Her forehead had gotten high and her hair was woolly and white. And she had a way of making her teeth clack as if she chewed on a rack of pork bones. She was sleeping all the time next to the blaring radio. I couldn't believe it. You've got to know my mother. I guess she wanted to hear something. Or she thought it would scare away robbers. Anybody could've come inside and taken her checkbook and her purse.

She had stopped eating. Her bottom teeth had fallen out and gone under the bed somewhere along with her watch. My mother's electrolytes were off. Chemically things were mixed up and she couldn't think straight.

The first day, I let my mother walk around and get things for herself. Especially since she left her checkbook out on the kitchen table under the window and open with all her bills scattered in amongst where we would eat, if we ate, where we would have our breakfast toast. But she wouldn't actually eat unless it was Enfamil.

Anyhow I let my mother walk and if she wanted something I wouldn't get it for her. In a few hours she was saying things like, "Well, I can't believe I am walking all across the room when I couldn't do that before you came." She'd act like it was impossible but if she wanted to be where I was she'd have to do it. She came and sat by me, each of us on lounge chairs by the TV with C-Span on. She couldn't understand any of it and when she'd read she'd hold a book to her face but you could tell she had wondered what this was in front of her. She'd get the crosswords out of the paper but I sneaked a look and saw she wasn't doing them.

She had been given a kitten and the kitten was wild, wild to have company and wild to have sanity for a change. Things are definitely going to get better with you here, the kitten thought. She bounced around the room. "Thank goodness you're here!"

I was wondering if we couldn't find a bite to eat and all she had was frozen macaroni. She hauled herself into the kitchen. We tried the macaroni. I put it in the microwave oven and it had a taste like steel. She ate hers though, clacking her teeth and sucking. I was glad because she was thin. She had a Dannon yogurt in the fridge. The date on it showed it was three months expired, but it hadn't been opened so I ate some of that. I'll never forget how she first came into the kitchen, showed me a wedge of cheese wrapped carefully in paper.

"I don't know what this is," she said.

A little later she showed me her Enfamil. "This is canned milk for people who don't eat," she said. "The trouble with it is that the cans have strong seals." My mother was too weak to pull the metal tab. I kept on getting up, sitting down, moving like an ordinary person but not offering to fetch things for my mother and she started getting stronger right away. In fact, that night she suggested we eat out. I couldn't imagine she'd have the strength to walk to the car but she did. She wore a pink suit with a jacket and put on lipstick and combed her long white hair.

That was the first day.

Aside from the chicken salad and the melon my mother ate everything on her plate. The waiter was Indian and we couldn't understand him and he wouldn't go away. When my mother paid him I said I'd do the tip but she bent over and got out her purse. Carefully with those long fingers all bent and with the nails cut straight across and working her mouth and clacking pretty loud she found what she wanted—a slip of paper from probably 1968 on which was printed a crib on how much to tip. Meanwhile I put out two dollars in change. She stared at it awhile. Then she shoved fifty cents back at me and tried to make me put it away in my purse. I put two dimes and a nickel back. She shoved the nickel again to my side with one long insensitive index finger. Now she felt she had it right.

We left the restaurant and went to bed and that was the end of the first night. I'd still not gotten anywhere much with her. She wasn't abandoned. She had her checkbook. Nobody had robbed her. But where were we? She was still no better off than when the con guy took her for four grand by selling her a new roof.

By the second or third day she was admitting things like, "I lost my lower bridgework. I think it might have fallen between the pillow and the mattress and the wall." And later she told me she'd crawled under the bed and found it. But not her watch.

She never let on she had a jigger in her bedside table but I saw it when she went to the bathroom. It was stainless steel. I didn't find the bottle.

There were lots of clues as to what was wrong with her. Always talking in the first person plural for example. And talking to the cat instead of to me.

"We are going to miss her, aren't we kitty? The kitty says she doesn't know what she is going to do when all this company goes away. You don't know what you're going to do, do you kitty?"

And not recognizing common objects was the worst of it. That was when her "electrolytes" were off. The day I arrived, she went to the counter and picked up a wedge of cheese, plain colored and hard. "I'm not sure what this is," she said vaguely. She held it up to the light, unwrapped it a little. It looks like it might be a block of wood—." She decided to taste it.

"I'd like to know the thought process that led her to taste a block of wood," my sister said. Then we had hysterics.

She found her nail file behind something. Who knows how long it had been gone? But her watch still hasn't surfaced. Here we are now well into late summer. We think it got burned when my sister burned the sheets. So she is wearing my dad's watch and it looks very funny on her. She looks like the kind of person who is dressed in somebody else's clothes down to the watch.

She hasn't taken a shower and she's still in double knit pants and tops now it's summer. She's pinning her pants, to hold them up, to her undershirt. She wears an undershirt now beneath her sweat shirt because she is cold, and little socks in colors like aqua and hot pink that match sweat shirts in the same color. This especially drives my sister wild.

And my sister charges me with the task of getting her to get her hair washed and cut. My mother is in a world of her own. She says she will look for the handle that fits the shower someday. Perhaps tomorrow. Same with washing her hair.

Next day we went over to the book store because I wanted to get a book. She sat down to wait at a table. Unfortunately it was near the topic, Sports. Nothing to look at but biographies of Magic Johnson. Nevertheless, she took that one and sat down with it. Slow motion. She takes her hands that I barely recognize anymore and opens it. Slowly she moves that index finger about as long as a pincher.

So while I was looking for the self-help books she is pretty settled. And when it gets time to leave we both exit slowly. I have to walk very slowly so she can keep up. And I'm driving the Olds. My sister has custody of it but said just for the trip why don't I use it. I'm supposed to sleep on top of the key so my mother doesn't drive again to the Party Shoppe. So my mother and I, we leave the parking lot.

We putt along and not far from it I see an alleyway. "It's an alley," I say. I am delighted. I haven't seen one of those for a long time, narrow, inviting, homey and people-sized. So my mother suddenly brightens up and she says, "That's my alley. I used to walk down that alley when I was a girl."

"Well, okay then," I say. "Let's drive down it."

So I go lurching slowly down the alley with the Ciera and there are no people of course, just some Sumac stubs with the red-green sprouts. "When we get to the end there will be our house," she says.

I've never heard this before.

"The house you lived in you mean?" I ask.

"My father designed it back before the Depression," she tells me.

I'd heard about that. We drive up the alley and there is a huge black shingled house with signs all over it, across the door, and on the porch as if it is commercial now.

"It is a frat house," my mother says wonderingly. She looks at the huge porch with the white trim and red Greek lettering all over it. She knows Frat houses, then, I think to myself. She can be really 'with it'. One time we asked her what to do about getting company to take left-over desserts home and she immediately said, "Oh heavens, husbands and wives don't eat dessert in front of each other. They won't take them."

"That's the same door though," she went on, looking over the house. "Over there is my grade school. And there used to be a field of daisies—. And we used to play there and then walk down the alley to the Grand River."

"Well," I say. "Things have sure changed. I should take a picture."

"There were cows too." She turns to look way backwards out the window. From my vantage all I can see is her pink scalp.

"Then we moved," she says. " —when I was finishing my last semester of twelfth grade."

The sun is shining. We drive, like two caged people, windows up, air on, in a sad town that is decaying, trying to imagine where the cows went.

Everything she had at home was either frozen or spoiling. The fact that she picked out some more cantaloupe at the store when we had a quarter of a melon in the fridge already was troubling to me. When she gave the cat canned food she left the opened can on the counter. She couldn't throw any food away.

"Throw it away for me," she'd tell us, because she grew up in the Depression. The only thing she threw away was coffee grounds. Before she stopped eating entirely she must have been eating frozen dinners and saving the plastic trays they came in. When I opened the stove drawer I found, this was a few days later, maybe fifty or sixty. At some point she stopped eating. I think that the frozen dinners after so many years got to be too much.

Besides being unable to throw things away she was unable to make phone calls or decide things or be active and do something such as lug her trash to the curb. It was a big problem. We would have liked for her to get rid of her magazines. They were *House and Garden* magazines. She was very uninterested in gardening. None of us had ever seen her do gardening. She was also uninterested in cooking. And she didn't do housecleaning either. Especially not now. That's why we had hired Mandy and Me not a minute too soon as my sister said. Not a minute too soon, she wrote me. My sister was really disgusted by the kitchen where my mother kept all sorts of cleaning bottles out on the counter but never used any of them. She kept little grey fuzzy pot scrubbers, and thin wafers of scouring pads. She kept rusting SOS pads and hung a towel by a hand-sewn handle my grandma made. Even if you used that towel over and over and were searching for another one, my mother would say you should use the one hung up. " —unless it's dirty."

The day came when my mother was much better but not entirely better. She was reading again and doing crossword puzzles in green ink. She was eating but she still wore the double knits and had long hair and talked through the kitty and got out of the lounge chair by putting her foot through the hole when it was extended. This was the way she had broken twelve ribs. (When she did it she got a funny look on her face because the doctor had told her not to.) If she did my sister was going to come and get the car and take it. By then it was banged up in several interesting places.

And then one day I called and no one answered. When I did reach her she sounded elated. "I took the car. I went down just to get some food that would be good to eat."

She wanted to drive to the store to get some chocolate sauce. Or maybe a mystery. She was vague about it. "I just got so hungry for a certain kind of ice cream," she said to me over the phone, but my sister and I thought: alcohol. The doctor continued to insist her electrolytes were still way off. She shouldn't drive. So we took away her car.

"Now that I don't have a car," my mother would say. "Since I am not driving," she might put in. "What with not having access to a car," was another way to say it. So finally the doctor said to her, "If you can pass the driver's test, you can have the car. The state will call and set up an appointment."

So she waited for them to call. Every day she would say, "I'm expecting a call from the state. The state hasn't called me yet." It went on for months. Every time I called she was expecting a call from the state. Any normal person would have called them but she couldn't. It was this business of the telephone. Hung up on her own phobias. It was really amazing. Life gets you in the end.

She has always been like that. She's got this checkbook on the kitchen table and it's all messed up. She stares at it. She owes all these telephone solicitors. She feels honor bound to pay all these charities twenty dollars. She doesn't know what her balance is. That's how the roofer got her. That and just plain taking checks right out of her book. So anyway she asks me to drive her to the bank so she can find out what her balance is. We get to the bank and I say, "I'd better let you out and park the car. But wait for me cause there are bad steps."

So she gets out and immediately I see her start walking into the bank, not waiting for me. She gets up the steps and stands in front of the heavy double doors. I try to park the car quickly but by the time I get out she is gone inside. Didn't even wait for me. I find her sitting in a chair and chewing on her tongue convulsively. But when she talks she sounds very normal. "I just wonder about my balance," she says. Very normal and then chews for a minute. The woman treats her like a mental patient, condescending just ever so little. It's Michigan apple pie politeness but it cuts.

Yet she doesn't appear to notice and when we leave she seems pleased. I go get the car. After all she's never really regained her ability to walk very far. She comes out. Without looking she begins acting like a person who has every right to be traipsing along in double knits, chewing on her tongue, scowling, and then, just as she gets to the car door and starts to get in it she pales and looks to see who's in there that she is getting in with. And for a minute she doesn't know it's me.

Earlier, we'd gone to the superstore and she selected a cart and just took off, her cart far ahead of me, as if she couldn't get lost. I watched her from a distance take two avocados and place them carefully in her basket. When I caught up to her she told me we needed sanitary pads.

I could say to her I'm afraid I'm a transvestite and it wouldn't faze her. I could tell her I've got a double set of permanent molars. I am entering into menopause and can't control my periods I might add. I fainted outside the movie of E. T. and both of my children were embarrassed and left me on the lobby carpet, and yet she's the one buying sanitary pads. We're all mixed up.

Kicks

I am trying to remember. All I get is the slit of an opening near the floor of the front porch. The porch floor is grey and cracked. I go there to play. I have a rubber ball and I lie on the porch and look through the vents at air and light and space. They are inside talking. They are tall while I am short. They wouldn't lie down on a porch, but I am tired. I am always tired of holding a posture. I want always to stretch and flop. It keeps me from being one of them, but I can't help it. Down there in the grass if I look closely there is a whole milky way of blossoms–how I love that small world.

I stick my foot gingerly into the slit of the porch. Has one of them ever done that? If I don't watch out I will get it stuck like the time I put the compact case in my mouth and it opened, and locked. I will get my leg stuck. It will hurt and my mother will think, what kind of a child is this?

It is very dirty on the porch. The railings are filthy and there are dust piles around each bannister. They are whispering about the war. My grandpa Messenger is in there talking on the telephone. My aunt Mildred, who can crack her gum, is crying. And what I don't know yet is that Uncle Irven has been shot down by machine guns on Okinawa. She is pregnant. I want to see the movie. I want to say something childish and selfish like, "Let me see the funny papers." I am truly a child.

But, I have heard of their war. I sit on the big chair in the dark and wonder if the fighter pilots can see the thin light in my living room during the blackouts, and whether they will consider it worth investigating. I wonder that the huge automobile plants in downtown Lansing don't attract their greater attention and then I know they have a movie too they want to see. But I cannot hold the thought of death, not even that of one uncle.

       ે   ે   ે

I don't know why, but when my brother and I are put to bed together we kick our feet. We only do it when we are given a big bed when we are visiting somebody. My brother and I both get terrible leg aches and colds and his eyes glue up if we don't get our sleep. We get into the bed, which is perhaps one of my grandmother's in the spare room, and into sheets that are cold and shocking as religion, and we kick and kick. It is exciting and we laugh. A bus rubs past the corner of the room and a street light pours in all night, vacantly. Doris-Mae's formals, peach and pink and lime, hang in place in the closet, finally not important; and we are just two small children in an iron bed. Over us hangs the war photograph. My grandfather has circled my uncle's head. Among all of them, this one is just part of a design, pin-sized. We kick and kick.

       ે   ે   ે

My father painted our basement floor so I could roller skate there. Pillars of metal in the basement helped me get up speed. I was an Olympic skater, an acrobat of most incredible grace and speed. Then, my father painted a shuffleboard court and made shuffleboard disks and pushers and the whole game. After that, he set up an electric train set. At first, it took only the furnace area; but finally the trains reigned all the way around. Plaster-of-Paris mounds of grey hills, and stretches of green, and houses, and towns divided the whole basement. He was fond of putting down herds of cows and collie dogs. Then the train ran through this most accessible country and sizzled and hooted smelling of electricity and painstaking brainwork on the part of Thomas Edison and my father.

       ે   ે   ે

When I look at Grandma Messenger this is what I see, I see backwards into her past. My grandmother has gray hair cut very short with waves over her ears. She had tuberculosis. Her fingers are ancient disasters. When I am old will I have those things? Broken bones in my feet? I look deep into her apologetic eyes, brown, into her mouth which is a cave with stumps. I see well into her past. I go down into Kansas; and I know the story she will tell me that once she had yellow hair.

She tells me one night it was so hot she got up, and took a horse–I have only a dim idea of what this meant–and began riding out on the prairie, prodding the horse to run until he went wild and she couldn't control him. Suddenly he turned and took her straight towards town and down Main and everyone saw her in a gown with her yellow hair, "the yellow headed Dane", only now it is mine, hair that reaches down to my waist, wild like the asparagus fern used to deck the church. I go straight out in my night clothes, the horse running away. Yes, I know–although I have never ridden a horse bareback, never been to Kansas.

                ಀ   ಀ   ಀ

The first deal I ever made with God, I was drinking a bottle of soda pop, a slick sticky orange, in the bait shop on Wall Lake. I was sucking on that straw, sipping up that juice that went right to my head. I was about ten and I made a deal with God to take my life in exchange for my youngest brother's. I delved down to the very last Bible story ever told me on a Sunday morning of my Presbyterian childhood.

But He didn't answer. I wouldn't have put it past Him to remember it later, but at the time, there was certainly no response. Meanwhile the alive and active God in the Bible I knew, made up of snakes and lions and caves and ravens, walls and bugles, and killing and coming to life, palms and donkeys and people unwrapping themselves from strips of cloth, tumbling alive, staring from the pages, always intervened.

But Red Angels came out of the nearest town, which was Delton, in an ambulance, and took my brother and they couldn't revive him; and I sat as if I didn't care, up at the bait shop, drinking my orange soda, solemn and unbroken, and He didn't break the silence either.

He's like that. Phone off the hook, gone to the store, day-dreaming, tending the goats, out to lunch, under the weather, in hospital, sick, laid up, otherwise occupied, occupying a ditch, waiting tables, talking baby talk.

In church, we sang about harvest and scattering ripened grain, none of it real. What I knew about was His silence.

≈ ≈ ≈

There were two girls who sat in front of me during Junior Church when we sang hymns and were treated to a shorter sermon than the grownups. There was a small theatre in the room with velvet curtains. The two girls always sat together; they even looked somewhat alike, (I sat behind them on a folding chair). They both had dark hair, pulled into barrettes, and brown eyes, and they wore plaid taffeta dresses and white socks and black patent shoes. First one of them would spend most of the church service tickling the other. Then they reversed. A delicious sound happened when one of their hands ran lightly over the shoulder blades and down the spine –I associate it with taffeta–up over the shoulders, down the back bone, out to the sides and back again. But all the while, they both looked straight ahead.

I did not let anyone know I wanted to be tickled and touched, never said, "I love you," or, "I am sorry," or, "Do you love me?"

I did not know how to fight for my rights (whatever they were), and I existed in a time frame of my own, feeling much pain, and if I were to ask **them** to touch me–my back or hair–and they forgot or stopped, I would not be able to bear it. I would not ask again.

≈ ≈ ≈

There was something about ice, about getting ice, about the tongs, the slippery floor. There was something about my mother's short black skirt, her white blouse, something that happened in the kitchen one time when my mother put a sign in the window that said, ICE. That morning I had been sent a grass skirt by my uncle from Okinawa that smelled of the grass where my uncle died, and one small folded letter.

Then all afternoon we waited for the ice delivery, until a man finally came and threw a weight down on the pavement to make the horse stay, and lifted a block of ice onto his back. He came into our back door.

"Why did he wink, Mother? Mother, why did that man wink at you?"

≈ ≈ ≈

Well, Baby Jesus, you look so old and so wise. I can't jump rope (more than two or three times) and I can't do a yo-yo. Baby Jesus, what do you think? How can you be so good? Tell me. And so wise?

Tell me how you can be so small and be held by your mother and yet be the savior of the world? I might like to have been savior of the world. If I stand on the hassock? If I recite the Wisemen's speech? No, no I fail.

At Christmas, my mother made red candles, great red candles with scrolls in them and chubby cherry-like shapes, short red candles she made, and that was a kind of saving. Saving the world–and I went to my nap singing "The First Noel," with a marble in my mouth and swallowed it.

The savior of the world singing a Christmas Carol with a marble in its mouth!

ᔧ   ᔧ   ᔧ

My hair makes a hoop and with it little no-see-ums play. It is summer and I am stretched out on a bank; no, it is a pier. We used to call it the seawall, at Lake St. Clair, where the Messengers live. My nose is pressed against the warm wood. It smells of sea weeds and the scorched smell of seawrack that has lodged in the cracks all bleached out like the no-color of my hair. I am unfledged, not a woman, but I am on the pier getting a suntan as they are.

I can see my mother, further down the line, lying on her back. She wears a one-piece suit. My aunt is wearing a bikini. Her flat blond braids are wrapped around her head. She, too, is lying on her back. But I lie on my stomach because I have goose-bumps. I have been swimming hard all morning and I want to soak up the warmth. The wet imprint of my body as I rise up to look at it blanches and wavers. Looking down past the seawall to the water, I see that it sinks sinks sinks while rising; I too want to embrace something, want to hold something stronger than my arms can accomplish.

ᔧ   ᔧ   ᔧ

They have taken me out on the water. They do not realize how they have transported me. I am not their child anymore; the waves bounce and take me into another world. I am not afraid, but I am in a new element. We are rushing through the water in the boat whose skin I feel beneath my knees. This is a new world but I am not afraid. Twisting black plants live beneath.

But my mother is not entranced. My mother and father do not fall into each other's arms and begin to make love, nor do they fall asleep. They resist. All this sea and its rocking, they resist it. My father quietly baits his hook. Oh, so patiently. My mother will not let-on that she is even alive. She sits as if sorry to be out with us in a boat in the middle of the morning and I am caught between them like a bulldog in the boat, sniffy and touchy.

They would not understand the words I want to put to the waves, hammer-cutters stone-cutters steeple-bells.

      ð   ð   ð

One time we took a train. (This was in Lansing, Michigan.) There was a train station. The whole experience was loud and mounting, the uproar of the train like fever dreams moving ever louder with increasing rhythm. Then the engine appeared, its wheel gear unimaginable the way it clocked and went round. And we, like little Russians with suitcases, my mother and I, on our journey–the massive strangers of the train experience.

The buying of tickets, the fear of something going wrong–no money, no ticket or the wrong time–then came the approach of those wheels, the step up, the next incredible step up. The possibility of miss-step. (But if she were doing it.) Then we were on board and sitting on the plush seats with cigarette burns.

The stewards' soiled uniforms; ah, Lansing was feeble. I amused myself looking at the other passengers, men who pulled their window curtains shut and went to snoring. What if one of them were my grandfather? Or what if I had been born black instead of white, what then? for railroads were the stuff of divisions. I remember a story I had read, about a mother and child going on a train to Detroit to see a white dentist, and that man refusing to treat them. But, my mother did not have to be brave or insist on her rights. Perhaps she was not brave at all. She was taking her little winking wedding ring that my father gave her to Grandma Messenger's house and I was going with her, that was all.

      ð   ð   ð

I touch the cherries on the brim. It is a black hat, very shiny with a coffee veil. I lift the turquoise Indian bracelet with symbols in another language. What do they mean? There is a deer and a sun with an arrow. I push on the hat. I slip the rabbit skin bathrobe over my head. I put the compact into my mouth, tasting the latch. It is a small rouge case. I feel it open and the hinge go click.

Ahhhh! The lid stays stuck and I am like a crocodile with a stick in its jaws. She rushes in and takes the compact out of my mouth. She doesn't ask what I was doing. I feel numb, numb as the cedar chest with its strips of blank wood. If I had been an Indian bracelet with the secrets locked inside the symbols, so much the better, the rabbit robe glowing orange in the closet, the hats for no one, the books, the radio, the bed with nubs that leave prints on my skin–soft red marks that eventually fade–and I fall to sleep with tears running down onto the spread.

Sometimes, in the afternoon I think of my brother, gone like a glance taken over twenty years; how he would have talked about this present world. He was a great talker, when I was silent. In the black mirror of the lake where my grandmother, our grandmother Messenger, swam after dinner in a black suit and an inner tube, he is my companion. We dive and play in the darkness around a rubber pontoon boat. She, meanwhile, is as naive and helpless as the moonlight is inhuman, a non-swimmer.

HOUSE OF SKY

John and I came to Crete to work in the University of Crete Library at Retimo or Rethymnon. I came to read and write there and John came on a sabbatical and as a library consultant. At first, we lived without a car, in town, in an office of the Administration building. The office had one room with twin beds and one desk and chair but there were high ceilings and a balcony that looked down on the garden of an old woman.

But where are the in-between women of my age? I find either old or young. Even now as I am passing a lace shop, a leather-goods store, a cobbler, I see the old women in black wool, forthright, forceful, and afraid of nothing. I could be their age. I too have earned the right to be in mourning. Suddenly though I turn and head toward the old Venetian Fortezza and find myself in a quiet sheltered lane bordered by jars which eons ago in Minoan times held oil, and come upon the overhanging balconies of wood, the gorgeous polished doors and handles, the colored shutters for the windows, and the sweetly singing song birds.

You might think the birds themselves are absorbed in their thoughts or trying to fill the transparent space around them with their small, unassuming bodies. Then you see the flutter, the small jump into air as they are awkwardly attracting attention. The more people gather around, tourists and so on, the less they sing. But these are the songbirds which can be found in any back garden and which old women keep.

Don't ask when you see them feeding the birds back there. They do it just in passing. They fill the shallow tin with grain, roll it around inside a while, let the sun catch in the edges, and then, lifting the cage, engage the feed niches.

It does them good to take care of a row of rabbits too, three to a cabin and hopping eagerly at supper, their ears falling about their eyes, their excitements contrasting with the black wool garments of the women, the slow steps the deliberate mouth.

But it is for the chickens, one white, the others black or grey and black, that the woman beneath us where we live suffers herself to cut a few greens, tossing one or two dried ones over her neighbor's fence, tucking the rest into the wire cage so they might peck at the horta. Even though a moment later these hens forget all about it again. There, the left hand takes a stalk of jasmine, pulls out some geranium, tamps down the bundles of twigs into a slantwise pocket. The sun moves into a slight angle, the old woman steps forward. There is a thrilling bird song, no one knows from where.

One morning I look down and see that the hens are loose. I cluck to the white one, boak boak! certain she answers me, her body an exclamation point. The sky is falling! Then the old woman, spreading her arms wide, comes like a hawk making a noise in her teeth and weaves about the terrace seeking young chickens. Wheezing wheezing she sings to them, warns them until she gets them all in.

Reemerging from the house she carries a cloth which she has washed and hung out to dry for years, shaken it, worried it against the white-washed wall so long it doesn't even know a hem. She goes back inside to the dark. The song birds, they find this quite sufficient.

      ॐ   ॐ   ॐ

"I prayed to discover my childhood and it has come back."
            —Rilke. *Notebooks of Malte Laurids Brigge*

One morning I woke and looked down onto the old woman's terrace. The cage was empty. The rabbits were still inside with round lids to weight their boxes but the hens had vanished, and they didn't return.

Later that same day at the open market I heard them, many many peeping yellow chicks in cages waiting to be sold. How? the crate? the dozen? the kilo? On top of one construction the seller has set up a single chick and around this one he cups his hand protectingly. I spy the larger hens too and rabbits on the ground also in cages. Do they belong to my neighbor? Of course, I can't tell. They seem unconcerned. They don't so much as look out.

      ❧   ❧   ❧

I was uneasy when the school children called after us, "Allo! Baby!"

When I heard the ducks start up at night I imagined a rat. I read the Serbs were being bombed by NATO forces yet the Serbian young woman who was employed by our friend, an older lady with reinforced silver teeth whose children were extremely successful, called to mind my failure to make something of Yugoslavia.

"She is very poor," cautioned the old lady in English about the Serbian woman, shoving her apparatus forward with her tongue. "But very gifted in book-binding. She can copy anything if you only show it to her."

The Serbian girl, who looked like a Botticelli, worked in what must have been a stable, in an archway where she could barely stand up. A table had been placed there and a bowl of paste with a large brush. All over the table were books finished and part-done, and behind were shelves of books with tawny leather bindings of all colors. There was a press and shelving and wastebaskets full of used papers and cardboard. The Serbian girl watched our faces and looked at us as we talked while smiling ever so slightly. Her voice was soft. Her father was with her. They had no country.

"She is so poor, and without a work permit," continued the old woman who owned the bookstore, "but she is so gifted, it is marvelous, really."

The bookstore which was charming occupied a space next to the bindery. There was a small desk, a table with books, walls of books and two stools with upholstered seats.

I was uneasy another time when I wanted to buy a loaf of bread. I had seen a man carrying a round bread under his arm, unwrapped, and I wanted to have one like it. We went into a bakery and I saw right away such a bread and took it to the cash register but as I laid it down I saw that it had writing on it. Is this special bread? I wondered. Is it okay to buy this bread?

And there was a hesitation in the baker which made me know it was not okay.

"Oh yes, of course," he said hesitating. "It is religious, but . . . ."

"I think," I said, "I would like a dark bread that is grainy that doesn't have writing on it." He found one for me from the back just out of the oven, for what would bread taste like meant for the altar or the hands of a priest?

        ಢ   ಢ   ಢ

"Nor shall death brag thou wanderest in his shade."

–Shakespeare

We went to the movies. It was a brilliant movie, one in which I covered my eyes and plugged my ears. Still, I knew it was brilliant, even funny. The brilliant movie treated death as a joke. A man's head was blown off because the car hit a bump. Then the persons who killed him had to clean everything up. They argued over who had the back seat.

We are each other's guests in Crete. At the library the women and few men who work there take us into their treasure: to teach me words, "You learn one new word every day." But a word dies with me each day. Words seem to curl like burning wood on the ends and smolder and become hulls. My effort to talk to people, my mixing up the word for 'stamp' with the word for 'stop'. the name Stavros with the place Stavros, the word for life 'zoe' with the word for animal 'zoo'.

There is a shaggy dog who lives in a drain pipe, and a goat's shed with sliding wood door. There are bins, feed pans, grain containers, plastic bags. But so used have I become to it all that my eye erases the sights I don't like. I love it here!

The houses are decorated with Cretan wood settees ornately carved in dark wood and covered with lace. Much is made of ornate embroidery. There are old trunks and leather framed mirrors. The beds are iron painted white. As to the sweeping of steps and terraces and the mopping of floors or beds that are turned down so the inhabitants sleep soundly in the afternoon, what of it? It is to put off death.

        ಢ   ಢ   ಢ

My sister wrote me from the USA saying. Your mother is aging very quickly. She is losing weight and now they say she doesn't answer questions.

It was too late to ask her the questions. Did Grandpa abuse you? Why was Grandma Messenger so cold? Did you love my father? Why do you drink? Why did the Depression grip you so tight? Why didn't you ever leave Lansing, even for a visit? Why don't you believe in God?

        ઠા   ઠા   ઠા

> "I write melancholy always melancholy: you will suspect that it is the fault of my natural Temper. Alas! no. –This is the great Occasion that my Nature is made for Joy–impelling me to Joyance–& I never, never can yield to it."
>
>   –*Coleridge #1609. notebooks. vol. 1.*

My mother is aging, so I call to mind a vivid picture of her at Christmas, standing on linoleum in the kitchen, evenings, and singing a Christmas carol, the warm breath rushing into the kitchen to stand like a cloud above the sink, my mother's homemade candles on the sill, the way she put a wick in each of them while the wax was wet, the difficulty to keep the wick standing–something I had not considered–propping the string and watching the wax grow, the languorous substance of wax becoming clay; and a day later seeing that it indeed held the string.

I would not have believed that also this was during the time of the Battle of Crete, the second World War.

> In the neck of the pass the fighting troops leap-frogged their way back...down through the innumerable hair-pin bends as the broken dusty road twisted its way down towards Sfakia. The columns moved at night. During the daytime the men slept among the boulder-strewn countryside, crouching in primitive shelters, in drainage culverts and in caves.
>
> "I would have wished," stated one of the soldiers of the evacuation on Crete, "to be nothing but a bird, I didn't even know what kind...."
>
>   – *Alan Clark: The Battle of Crete*

As I write they are playing soccer in the street. The men from the town where we now stay, Gallou or Gaul, have let the little brown dog run loose. The dog who lives in the drain pipe. The dog runs in the road with the father and children trying to catch the soccer ball. The father lets the dog catch it. The dog puts its paws over the ball. The father pretends to kick it away. The dog's tail wagging, the dog runs for the ball again. When a truck goes by the father bends over to hold the dog, and also he waves at the driver.

The children build a small fire in the schoolyard. The little girl who is four is with them. I see her reach up. Then I hear church bells. It is twilight. Night falls on all of this. December 11th.

And now I think again of Coleridge's statement about being happy. "This is the great Occasion that my Nature is made for Joy–impelling me to Joyance–& I never, never can yield to it."

❧   ❧   ❧

Letters

Your letter reached me late the week of Thanksgiving and I was happy to get it. We have lived in a hotel in Athens, another two in Crete, a village called Gallou, found no heat, no hot water in the kitchen and moved to a one room office in the administration building in town in Rethymnon. Stayed there one month waiting for money, a free car, something. Finally I thought John would leave me/go crazy so we moved back to Gallou again, rented a car which by this time, season being over, was much cheaper. It is a Mirabella, grey but has power enough to climb the steep hills. So back in Gallou I am getting adjusted. We heat water for the kitchen or draw it from the bathroom sink. We bought an electric heater. I like it more and more each day. Two porches look out on the lives of the largest assortment of animals you can imagine. I feel as if someone gave me a writing fellowship.

Dear C.

It is Thanksgiving Day and mercifully, no one here knows it. We can nurse our American feelings alone although John did try to explain the holiday to a library staff person who nodded and said, Yes, it was about the eucharist and catholica. After that he gave up. The words 'pilgrim' and 'indian' come to mind along with 'squash' and 'feathers'.

Dear L.

I have seen the Greek Orthodox priests in tall hats share a confection of sugar and chocolate. I crawled into a cave that had a blanket in front of it and stacks of prayer candles and icons of tin like very thin cookie forms. Inside the cave, it smelled of incense. The frescoes had the eyes shot out of them by the Turks. There were bay leaves around the doors as if the church had been granted a laurel, and immense ornate sensibilities instructed the decoration within. I thought of Elizabeth Bishop whose "Protestant self shuddered".

Yorgos next put us in his van and took us to a remote village where we walked to a Byzantine church, one of the 600 on Crete that contains ancient frescoes, and I stared into the brown startled eyes of a male or female painted upon the wall. Then we left, stared at the rusted bell gaping in its irons, and walked down through the village taking figs, opening the skins and eating them, pulling oranges off the trees and eating them, and twisting off the little pickles on the plant that spits.

Dear Olivia

Your father is leaving for Thrace, a town very far away but still in Greece. It is on the mainland. Here in Crete it is called Thraki. And from there he will take a bus for four hours to a place called Xanthe. Dad thought he was leaving on the boat this evening and we prayed this morning for those who travel on land and in the seas. But late in the day it was arranged to have him go tomorrow at six by plane from Iraklion to Salonicka and thence.... Dad all but had his skin patch on when he heard that. It was cold for several days, the little children appeared in snowsuits. Then today the weather turned fair and I went swimming. The strange thing about Crete is that the tourists are all gone now. The majority of the tourists come in large groups of arranged tours on tour buses. The fragility of this is that if the tourists next year should become fickle and decide Crete isn't so much fun after all, they will go perhaps to Malta. A taxi driver turns down near the sea and Dad groans and says 'ochee' (no) but the driver doesn't understand and then Dad says, "Well, are you just going to sit there?" to me. So I rally and say the word for 'post office' when I mean the word for 'stop at this station'.

❧   ❧   ❧

Prophecy, the form of language that forever eludes political control–In December if the moon is full when the weather is warm, it will be warm until the next full moon. If you sail in a boat which is unnamed, it is bad luck. If you dream, there is some truth to it, even if it is truth wrong-side out. Somehow, it is still the truth.

I called the sky in Crete 'House of Sky'. Some of the houses on Crete, it is true, are unroofed, thus, filled with sky. But that is not what I mean. When you walk up until you are in the highest place, the height of a village, then you are near it. Today the sky smudged itself very dark, like a cloudlet of purple everywhere.

Yesterday it hailed. We saw the stones on the porch. The dogs yowled. They did not know if they should go into their dog houses. The house of sky was coming down to them in these glassy pieces.

An old woman, one of the ones like I am going to be, comes out of her peeling green door–shocking green, the color of a boy's boat. She comes out wearing a scarf, carrying a pan of something. She fusses here and there. The sky reaches down to her pan and sucks up the water there. She spills it. Backs into the house again. The old woman pulls this sky into her bundle and ties it tight with a firm grip. The wind is a good wind today, not the wind from Africa, which in the summer causes headaches and craziness.

Epilogue

In Minos's garden, that is to say, on the island of Crete, they asked themselves that evening if they knew a holy man or if it were necessary to go to Mount Athos.

"And he says we must find a holy man, if we find one holy man we should ask that man to pray for him."

"Yes," he said. "And I have been worried about that."

It hadn't occurred to her. But it was his brother after all. "...that he may pray for me and I may stop behaving stupidly." That was what the letter to them said. Plus a piece of news about some French terrorists and an unnamed writer.

"What did he mean by that, do you suppose?" she asked. 'That he may pray for me.' Do you suppose he meant seriously? I think he did."

A little later she said, "A thought has struck me." But she said no more about it. She was on a writing fellowship. She could write all day every day. There was plenty of time.

The next day was not a Sunday afternoon with men and women attending church and visiting back and forth for the village; it was an ordinary working day with all hands churning out the beton or cement for new houses in the village, new second stories to existing ones, new hotels. All along the road up to Sto Galou the cement mixer trucks, pickup trucks and crews of men were in furious activity to the chorus of barking watch dogs. A brilliant sun dispersed the wind from the North and dried up the rain.

And yet long before morning had fully dawned she had received an idea on the wing. They would go to a church and light a taper for his brother and in this way fulfill the obligation. The idea was so strong that she cleaned her house before nine, finding hot water for dishes and clothes, a broom for last night's peanut shells, sacks for rubbish.

"Mr. you are to prepare yourself for this new day," she announced to him who had not received the rumor, at least not yet.

"I had an idea which struck me this morning before even I got up," she said to him. "We might go to the little village church in Galou and light a taper for your brother and also one for each of our children."

He cocked his head, sighed, but said nothing. Breakfast had not begun quietly enough for him and he was used to the slow dawning of the sky, a gauge of cloud and sun, a temperate roll toward the windows just so, hot shower, and then getting dressed in plain clothes to the accompaniment of Chopin's nocturnes very quietly.

A sharp, pale morning, wind blowing from Africa, slanted sun at this time in the morning upon the old Venetian stones. She always tried to decide the color. Brown? Ocher? Reddish white? No, the color of sheep's wool, not white, not brown either, but worn almost mellow. Squinting, they got into the car.

The church in Galou was accessed by going round the farms and coming down through narrow channels at steep grades, or by going through the old center, again through narrow roads and up steep grades. As they drove, they passed a donkey with a man on it sidesaddle going to his olives and joggling along with a rhythm. It was Dimitrios they discovered, when they turned around, not an old man. He had turned his truck over twice on the road to Rousso Spiti and so, rather than buy a new one, or sell some land—a thing no Greek would want to do—he was using his donkey. Things are never what they seem.

They stood outside the church under the fir trees which had grown very tall, very quickly too. Their faces were green veiled and shielded. But they found the door locked. They had already remembered anyway that they lacked a lighter.

"There is also the chapel on the way out of Galou," he said. They stopped at the second church in Galou, which stood out in the open fields and was circled by a walled courtyard of urns and white burial crypts with little chapels upon them, lighted from inside, decorated with Byzantine portraits, modern portraits, plastic flowers, and even, in several cases, bottles of soda or cans of Sprite.

"You go check if the door is locked," he said.

There was an iron gate with a latch. She turned it and it opened. Once inside a dim interior revealed the altars, icons, byzantine paintings, even a microphone attached to the pulpit where a green light rather like the bull's eye in a port-lid was glowing; and she found the altar table with orange tapers. Next to it was a money box and a lighter.

"So here we are," he cried, coming in, but softly for now he liked this idea. They both went up to the tapers, he putting money in the box, and began to light three of them.

The lighter scratched but wouldn't spark. "Damn!" she said, "Oh. Sorry."

"Hold the wick close and let me see if it will catch."

"It won't light," she said as she tried it again.

"It will not. No use."

Reluctantly they turned aside. "Damn!" she said again, and, again, "Oh, sorry!"

They felt like trespassers at any rate. The Greeks make the sign of the cross by putting three fingers together and moving right to left three times in a kind of motion suggesting a wide-slung cat's cradle which is different. The paintings on the walls made no concessions to Western perspective or humanism. All this creates a feeling of dizziness.

"Oh," he said. "The church on the square in Rethymnon. Either the chapel or its main church will have tapers and be open." They sped downtown.

"You go first," she said, "because here in Greece it is the men who lead." She was a little disgruntled. He crossed in front of her and walked carefully up the slippery white marble slabs which in town were still quite wet. Inside they could see many tapers already lighted in a pinkish-orange glow and he took three and began to light them from the others. She took one extra. "For Gloria," she said aloud, meaning for their deceased, eldest daughter, and finding a light for it walked entirely around the urn which held the lighted candles until she found a space where she might place it so it could burn. And not genuflecting, not bowing, she closed her Protestant eyes and in blackness sent up a prayer for each of them.

   ð   ð   ð

The next day was Paraskevi, a saint's name, Friday, and it brought countless duties for Kyria Tsirimonaki: the raking of the courtyard so that marks showed, the restowing of what old newspapers she could reach–some of them had slipped behind the Cretan settee, the mending of a cushion, new amethyst candies in the crystal dishes in her sitting room. Then she stood fussing, contemplating the table all set. Could it seat six in moderate comfort? Did it need the extension? Her anxiety about these guests remained.

Once she had looked down from her second story, on a rainy day, and seen some tourists in Rethymnon out of season, cold and wet. And she thought, "Oh, how I wish they might know what the real Rethymnon is, and not just the fancy hotels. And how sorry I am that they probably don't know anyone. And isn't it providential that they should be washed up upon my very kerb? I shall ask them in."

They might have thought she was making fun of them–she had inquired would they like to have some tea. They replied,"Oh no, never, no no, we are quite fine. We are not lost. We know exactly where we are." They had repeated that phrase. "We know exactly where we are." But the refusal! It was unheard of.

Hampers of soft cheese, the cream cheese called misithra, barley bread (the urban Cretans preferred this country bread) horta with the red and white roots attached, lamb, potatoes yellow and firm: all this was in the door.)

"What's the third bundle?" Mrs. Tsirimonaki asked Sulla, her youngest daughter. It was molded rice, spinach pie, tangerines, wine, cheese pie with honey.

"You brought the wine?" Sulla often forgot things, or broke them.

"Not all the bottles," she replied defensively, "which two broke, but all but two, of the white."

Kyria said nothing but she sighed.

   ð   ð   ð

" —does it not refer to the Cretan Regnum?" began Yorgos speaking to a soft-spoken woman scholar who was studying Renaissance

Crete, specifically Renaissance gardens of the Venetian occupation. He cast his eye quickly around the library to see if Maro was anywhere nearby for she spoke well and could be counted upon. As for him, he must see to an important telephone call and several other matters. This was, at any rate, the day he and the Americans were going to Kyria Tsirimonaki's dinner at eight.

His own Maria was not coming. She had no English, unlike Maria Tsirimonaki. Perhaps, then, he would not even go home. His brown knitted vest, grey and white stripe shirt with rolled sleeves, his greenish serge pants, and black loafers, would serve.

❧ ❧ ❧

At fifteen hours, John noticed a twinge in his abdomen. This caused him no little grief for he was given to such things. Indeed when he had locked himself in the bathroom the only comfort had been that at least he had his pills in there with him.

At sixteen o'clock he decided to take one of the large muscle relaxers which were very potent, and then lie down and take a nap. This he did but several times was awakened by a sharp twinge. At seventeen hours he told his wife what was up, that he didn't feel really very well. She was bewildered because she was a person who never got sick. He hated to tell her. She would want to know where and why and what he had eaten.

He decided to go out for a walk. It was almost dark. He would feel better to walk it off. He said, "Be so good as to put on some logs so that when I get back we can be cozy until it is time to go to dinner."

Considering that he had been lying on his side in the bed, clutching his groin, she was not entirely free about letting him go and when he did not return at seven, 'her' time, she had to fight down the images which came to mind of a dying man alone where prickly Cretan vegetation and limestone competed. But she won the battle and was comfortably reading when he came in at about seven-thirty.

He was not any better. He went directly to bed and at that point anger rose up in her throat and she told him perhaps he would want to go to the nosokomeio, before it got too late, before they entirely missed the chance to go to Mrs. Tsirimonaki's for dinner? She wanted to go there so badly!

Mrs. Tsirimonaki had invited them once before into her home just because they had come into her bookstall. It was a real Cretan home, elegant, Venetian, with stables, court, upper spacious rooms overlooking the sea. She found watercolor scenes of Crete by Edward Lear. Oh, how excited she was to see them. She had just read that the originals were in the Grenadier Library in Athens.

"There was a book published of them," Mrs. T. said to her and these are just copies, not the originals. "I think Edward Lear was very ungracious. He said some things about Crete that were unkind even though he was treated very well. Very well." John suddenly recalled a description Lear had written about traveling in Crete where he observed that his host "killed fleas with a tea kettle."

ے ے ے

John asked would she go across to the mini-mart in the village and use the phone? She should call Yorgos and ask him to meet us at the nosokomeio, in order to translate.

"Orieste? Pos? Malesta? Yorgos!" Maria answered first and when Yorgos came to the phone she explained that John had a pain.

"Oh, that is bad because we must go to Maria's house," he said. "She will have prepared a lovely big dinner for us."

"I know. I know. But he says he needs to go to the hospital."

"The hospital?"

"Yes, he has a pain. It is in his groin."

"It is going?"

"No. It is in his lower intestine. His stomach. I don't know where. He says he wants to go to the hospital and could you meet us there. We will leave right away."

It was a rainy evening in Rethymnon, quite dark, just after Christmas. Crete does not make much of that day in decorations. There was a small tinsel tree in the lobby. Yorgos could be seen waiting just inside the emergency entrance. A man full of fluids was being rolled in just then on a stretcher. The nosokomeio was freezing, to stretch a point, and the door was wide open to the night. Several other people waited on chairs facing this open door, most notably a young man with an extensive leg cast and no sock.

A water cooler in one corner had leaked and a puddle was forming on the floor which created a barrier everyone had to cross in order to gain entrance. A cleaning woman in scuffs and a grey dress with white apron, ran a mop through it from time to time.

The signals were polite, but brief; the doctors wished them to remain seated, there was an emergency situation in the examining room, the doctors were extremely busy there, a man had died, or was dying, or was likely to die, Yorgos wasn't saying for sure, and so they parted company, he going inside to that room while the Americans stayed waiting by the front door.

This waiting gave them time to hear the Greek tongue. Usually they were spoken to in adequate English by everyone from shopkeepers, especially shopkeepers, to school children. Now, however, she at least wished she had come here earlier, a few months ago when they first arrived, in her visit in order to learn the rudiments of the language for there was much greeting of the 'how are you?' 'and you?' 'how have you been?' 'and you?' sort. She knew this because she had mastered some of it herself. She never ceased to be amazed though at the vocal inflection, so different from American or British. 'Yes' was spoken as if you had picked a fight with the sentence before. "Neh" (yes) the Greek said. "What, do you want to make something of it?" he might have said.

A young woman in a tight short black skirt and stacked boots began to walk through the door. She saw the reflection of water, paused, with the glassy stare of one who has had some wine, and walked bravely, even elegantly, across it without falling. The man with the cast hopped through the water with his one good foot. The cleaning woman rolled out a cart with a wringer on it and made a fine display of putting the mop into it and wringing it out, dipping the mop into sudsy water. She stuck her head into the room where the relatives of the man in the emergency room had gone.

In a few minutes a stretcher emerged with a person on it beneath a white sheet. It was the man with fluids in him. Yorgos says, "His relatives are going to have to wait, and those who are still celebrating at the Cretan wedding, and don't know, they are going to have to wait until the weekend is over to have his body back because they don't know he is dead. He must be seen by a pathologist. Everything must be certified as to how that man died and when." Yorgos thinks he died at the wedding.

When John is called and they have examined him they ask in English, because Yorgos is at that moment down the hall, "What is our word for 'fat'?" They want a reduction in John's fat intake. Once this is done, there will be less chance of another appendicitis attack, which is the diagnosis. But they say,"Come back in one hour after some tests have been made. And take your temperature twice in the night. Wake up and take it. If it is elevated or if you have intense pain, return immediately."

Yorgos thinks that there is time, during the one hour wait, to go to Kyria Tsirimonaki's as planned. "You can't eat, John," he says, but your wife and I will eat something and we can tell Kyria what has happened. She will be worried about you."

ટ*   ટ*   ટ*

John snoozed and yawned outrageously. He did this when his brain wasn't getting enough oxygen. He could not be witty. His jaws snapped and his eyes ran. Sometimes he sneezed. He was dressed in pants with spots on them, he had forgotten a jacket. He was shivering. They were at dinner, the only dinner they would have, in Mrs. Tsirimonaki's kitchen, he with his feet near the caldron of smoldering olive pits, a Greek heater, she and Yorgos at the table eating potatoes and meat, then cheese pies dribbled with honey. Then tangerines. Then horta pies. Then water. Then–

Mrs. T. brought out the exact meal she had planned for them and it was still warm. She cut into every dish just enough to spoil it. It was too late at night for her to speak English. She chattered on and on in a fast Greek tonight. She also stood on stools too high up or crawled around among cupboards, and stooped down to find something near the floor. Finally Yorgos raised his leonine head from his dish to declare that they must leave.

ટ*   ટ*   ટ*

For many years he had kept a diary. He wrote in it the weather, music he would like to hear, how his stomach had been, whether or not he had slept well. It was always in shorthand:

Tues. Jan. 10. 1995. St. Matthew's Passion or Gorecki. Dinner with Mrs. T. A treat. She went to Ole Miss in the early '50s. Get her a book on Oxford. Appendicitis attack. Huge amount of discomfort and pain. She fixed all her dishes, couldn't serve them as new another time, I sat there yawning while they filled their chops. Debated what to do. I had said Let's not go but Yorgos said we ought to. And had she not put it away? and I was probably going to have a ruptured appendix.

ॐ ॐ ॐ

"That was an interesting night," Yorgos exclaimed with gusto. "A very funny night with a huge lump of a man there dead in the hall."

"What?" said his wife.

"I went in and that man was in there with several doctors and in addition he had some relatives with him, three men. Those people made a telephone call, right there in the room. I listened to them. Before they made the call, they agreed among themselves to say that the man had not died. They called the wedding guests, which was where he was at the time he felt ill, and they said, 'He's comfortable, I'm looking at him now.' All the while the man is dead."

"What?" she asked him, not ready to believe.

"What they said was: 'We have him here at the hospital, the doctors are looking at him now, they are doing everything they can.'"

"And then finally they covered the man with a sheet," he went on, "and wheeled him out with that huge stomach on him. And there were some other relatives of his sitting there and a man came up to them, another man quite unrelated to the incident, who was visiting the hospital for another reason. Seeing this, he came over, the man who didn't know he had died. This man said: 'Don't worry, you are in good hands, this is a very good doctor. I know her. and a good hospital. This hospital has everything. It has oxygen. Don't worry, you are safe!'"

ॐ ॐ ॐ

Besides being a librarian, Yorgos was a farmer. He was headed that evening to his vines. They were high in the mountains. He reached them just as the sun came within a compass point of dipping behind the Silorites Range. A pack of dense clouds drifted across. As if conformed to the shape of a funnel, vultures hung circling, circling, sucked up and down invisible shoots.

A draft of cold air came through the ravine between the mountains. It felt good. He noted from this distance all the natural caves and monkish apertures in the limestone.

ॐ ॐ ॐ

The morning drizzle was scarcely yet lightening but Mrs. Tsirimonaki could see that the Cretan Sea was going to slate today and the shore towards Iraklio was smudged and fogged. There was one white fishing boat out and nothing else. The Americans had knocked at her door last night exactly one hour late. She had let them in and with customary hospitality refused to let them go, they must come inside, must have something to eat, must come up. Once there, she ushered the sick man to a chair in the kitchen near the coals, and sat his wife and Yorgos at the table. But her dining room so elegantly set for six people down to the wine glasses and the silver was not to be.

It would have been wonderful conversation, she thought, as well as food, but it was not to be. Was this the reason for her ill-humor?

By mid-morning the wind had shifted into the west-south-west, and boats by the score hurried out, making it clear she thought that time was short. Towards eleven o'clock she had the house back, orderly, not prepared for a company of six in the dining room. Her domain grew larger.

She went downstairs and unlocked the door to the book shop, listening as she did to the important sound of the lock. It was a lovely book stall, just a niche, with a heavy drape over the arch, and bookends made of acantha leaves, corner stones from the old town. In addition, books and bills stretched before her as if gently undulating on sands in the morning sun.

"There's the doctor," said Zora coming in, smiling pleasantly. "And how was dinner?"

"Pah!" she said laughing. And suddenly Kyria Tsirimonaki experienced the complete sensation of freedom.

₰   ₰   ₰

They were experiencing island climate, very changeable. This was the Cretan winter, wet, damp, and right now, quite cold. The wind came from Chania, from the west, when it did not come from the north. Now if the wind would only shift to the south — but it did not. The Cretan Sea bore white caps crashing shoreward. It was the color of a frigate. Or was it the color of the Mississippi when the light lay just under the surface grazing every ripple?

Every day the Americans had used the same coffee mugs bought when they arrived. Dittany tea was made in them which was pale green and good for digestion. White-hot raki was taken from them as well, and orange juice every morning before coffee. By Christmas they were dipping the holiday biscuit/cake in the coffee before she wrote in the afternoons. And each time, the mugs were washed either in the summer house or in the bathroom of the office building.

"You know what I am going to do?" John said.

"What?" she says.

"Smash my cup. I am going to throw it into one of the ravines."

There were so many ravines but one of them would do. They did throw them.

"Ah," John said, "music–God's intervals."

They heard the satisfying sound of a crash, his and hers.